DEDICATED TO JOE

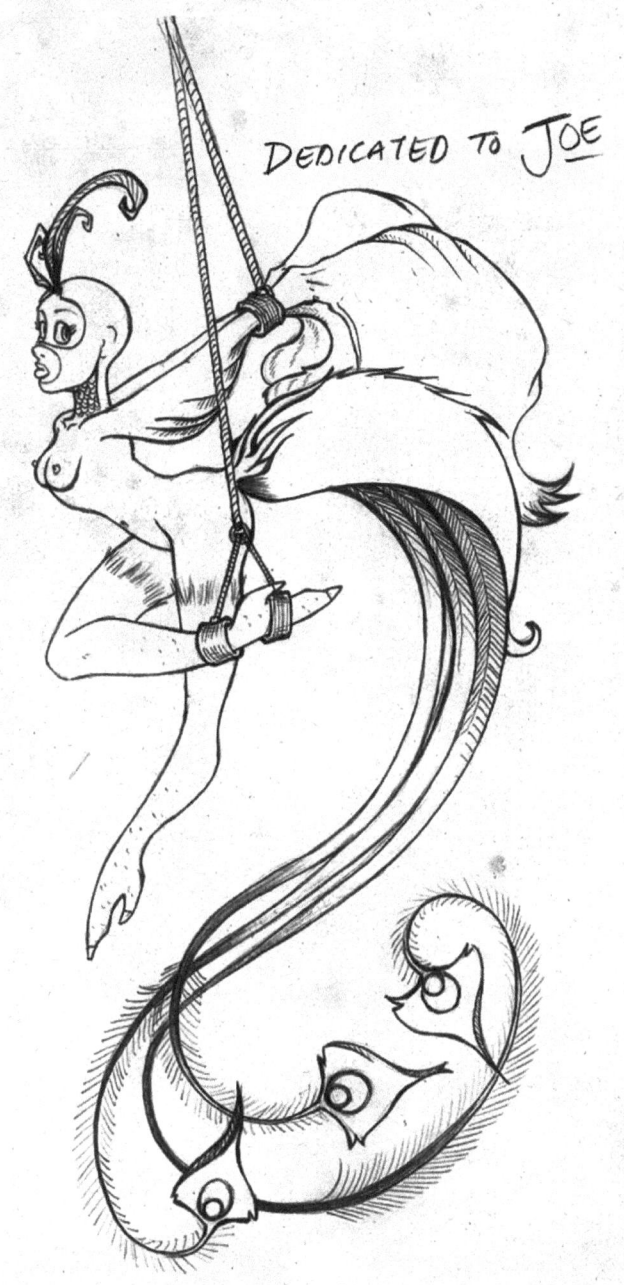

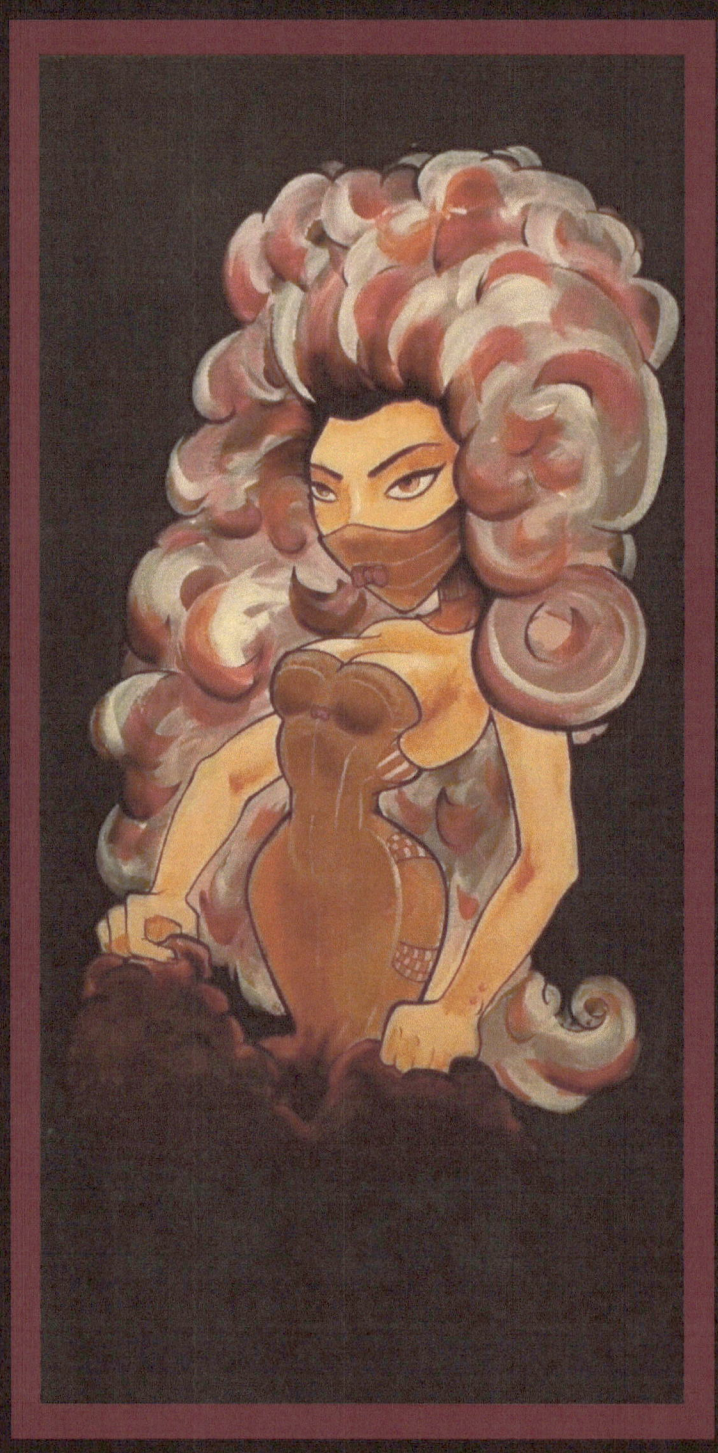

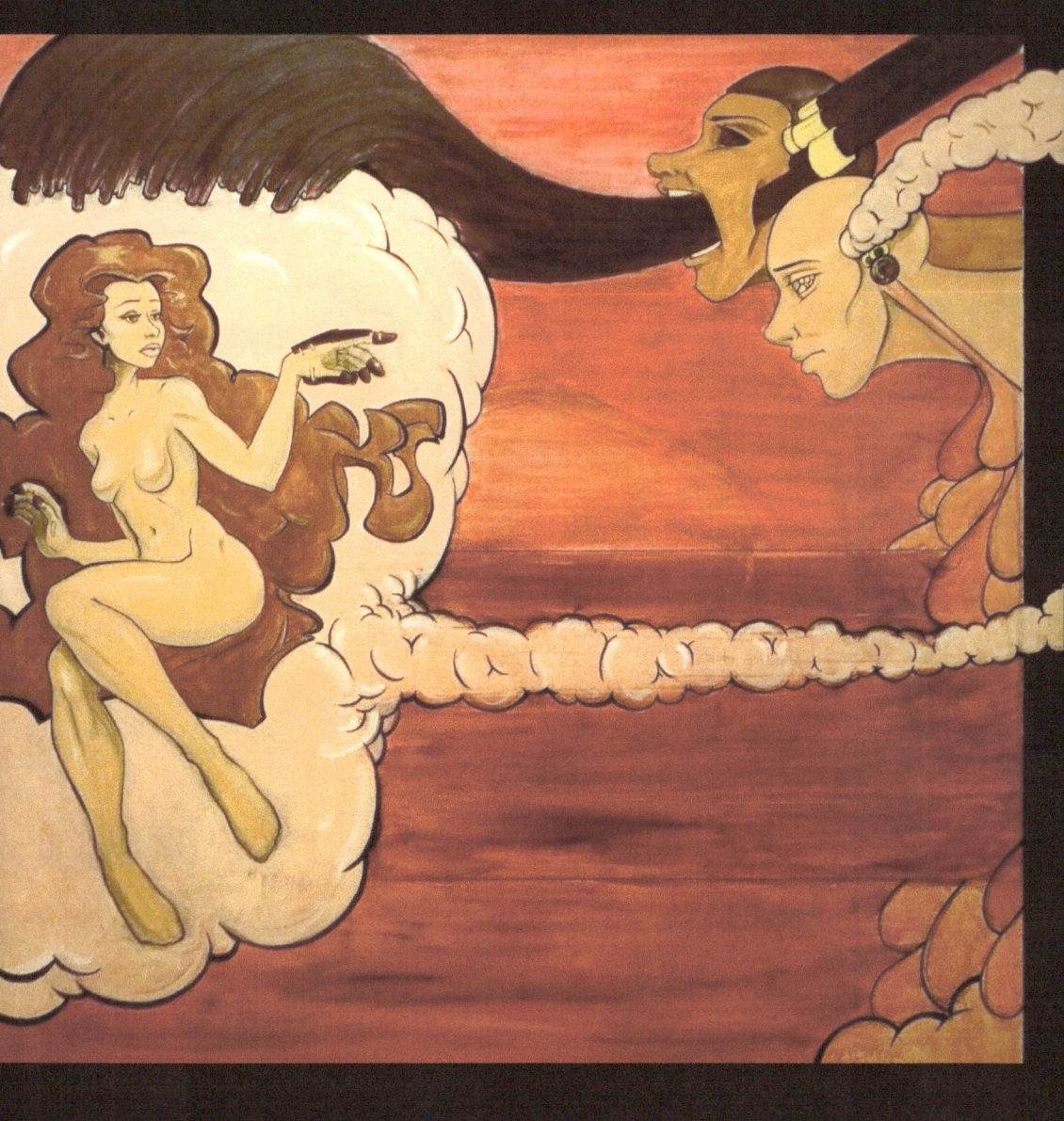

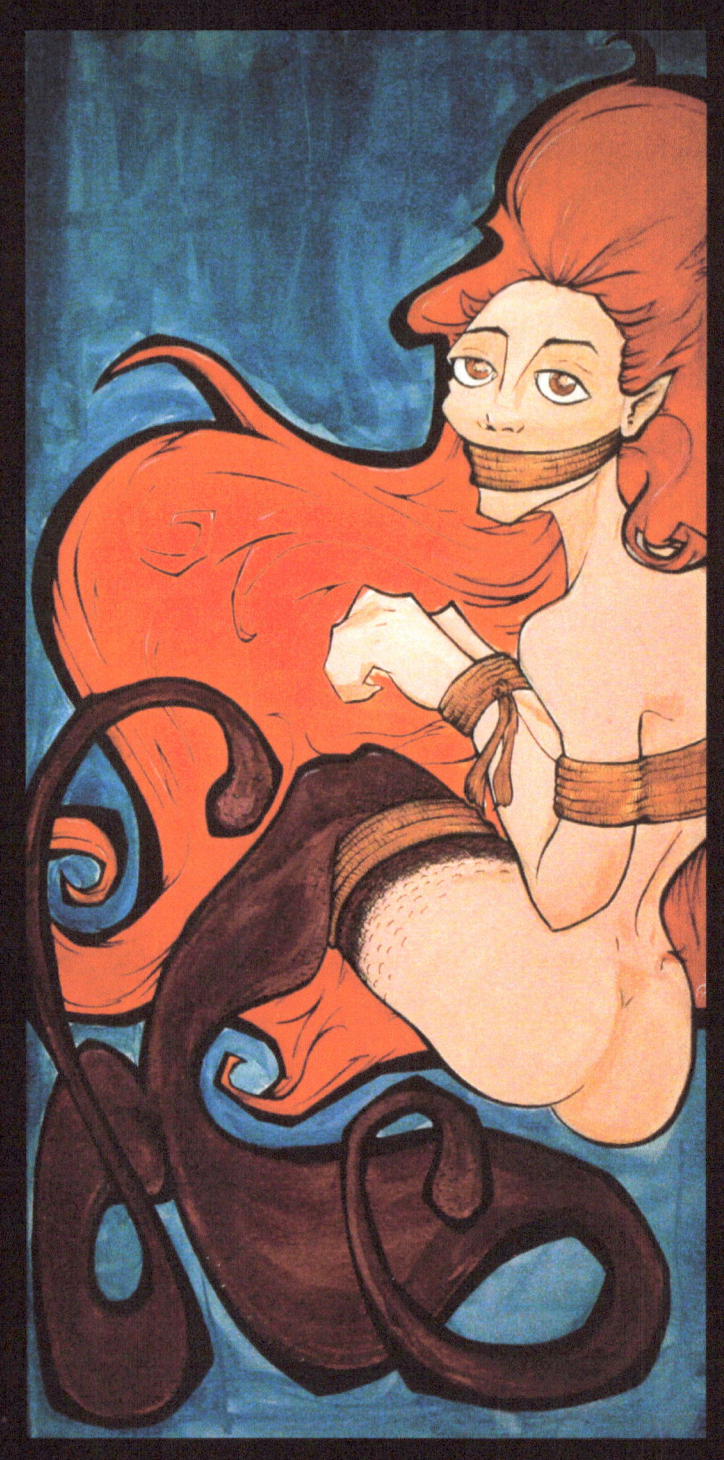

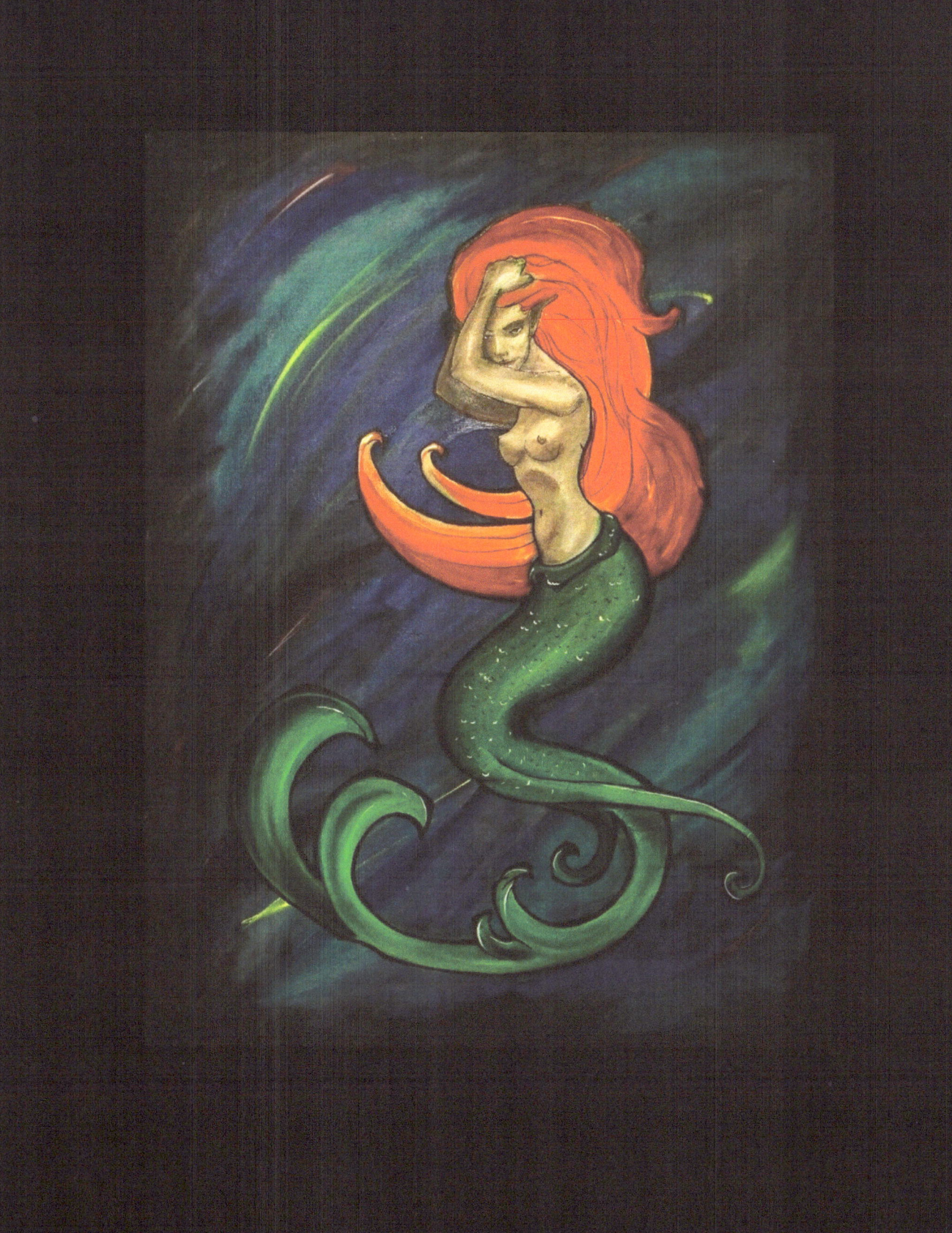

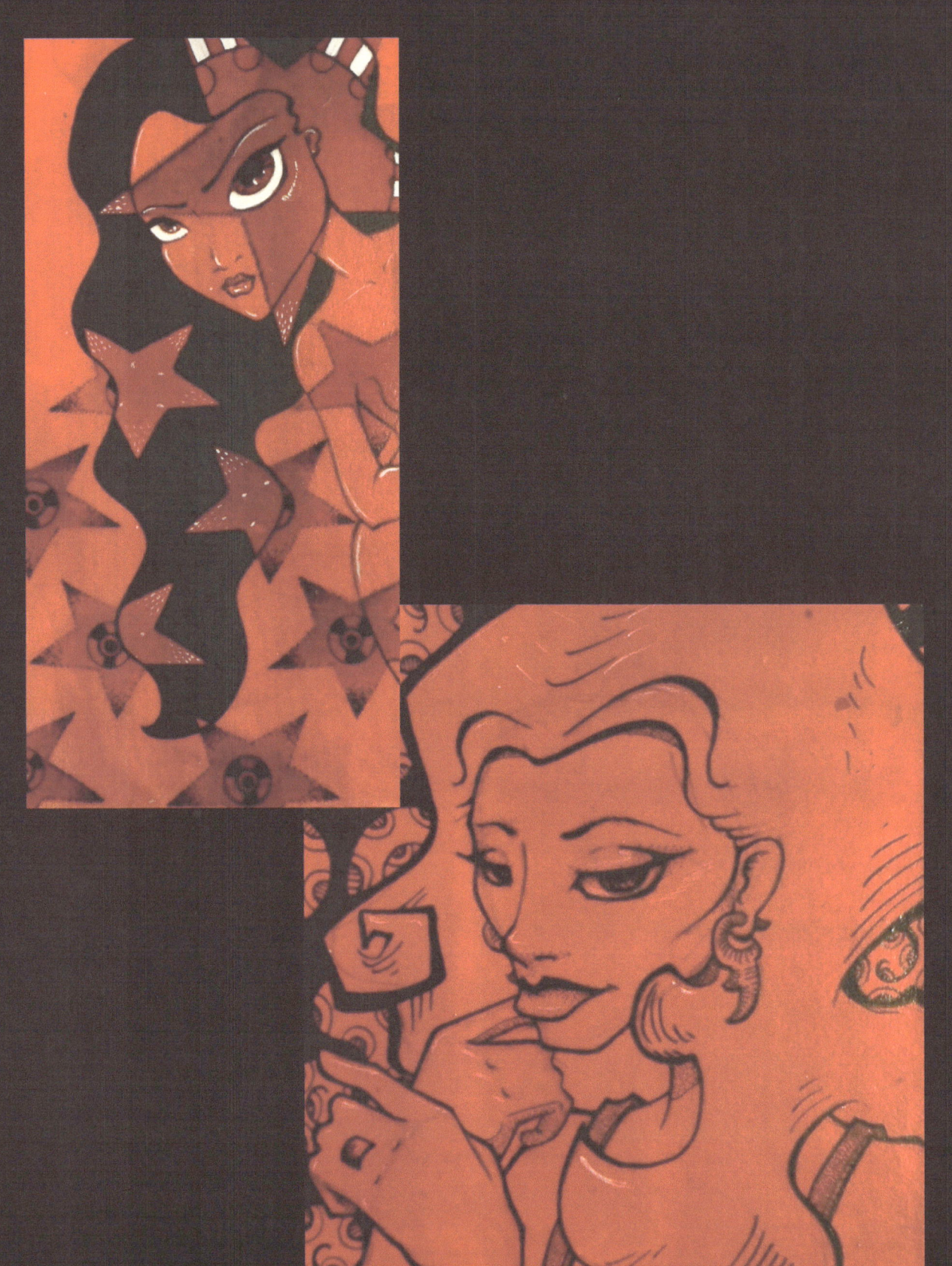

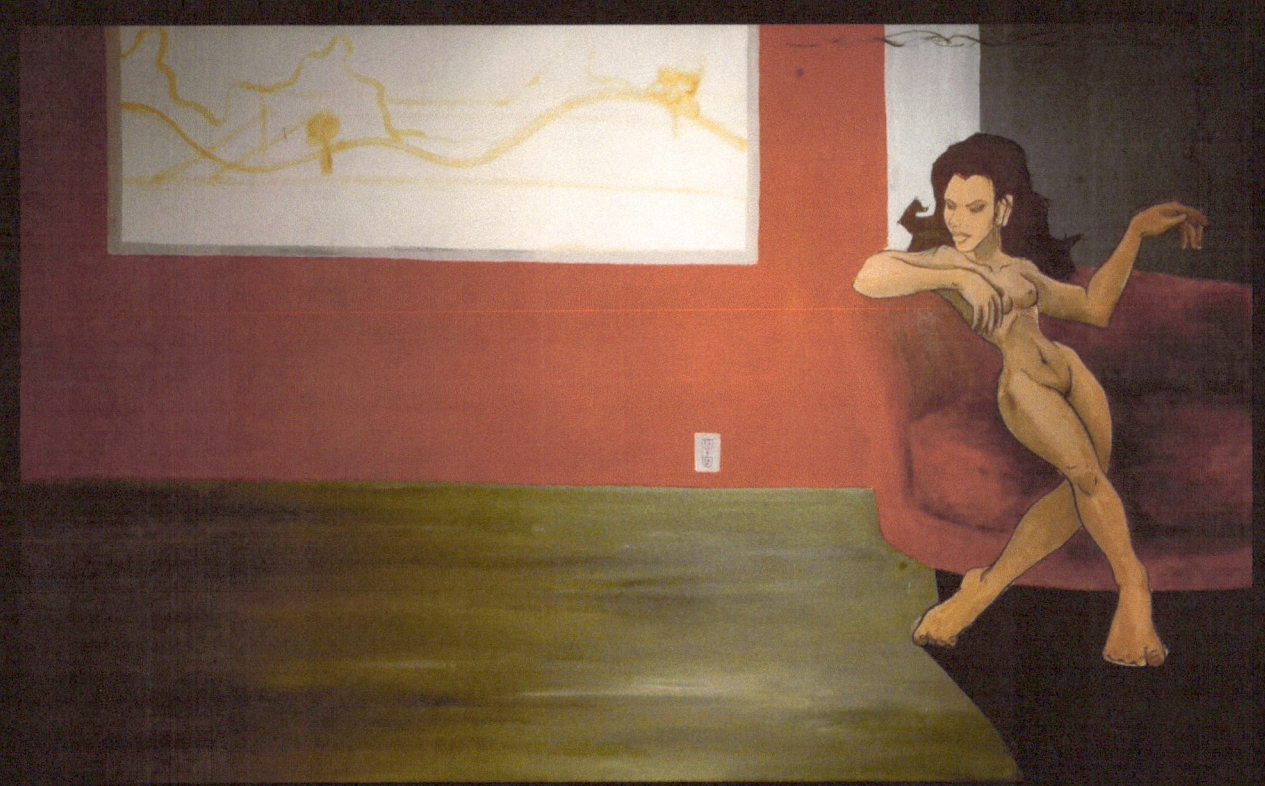

WORK IN PROGRESS

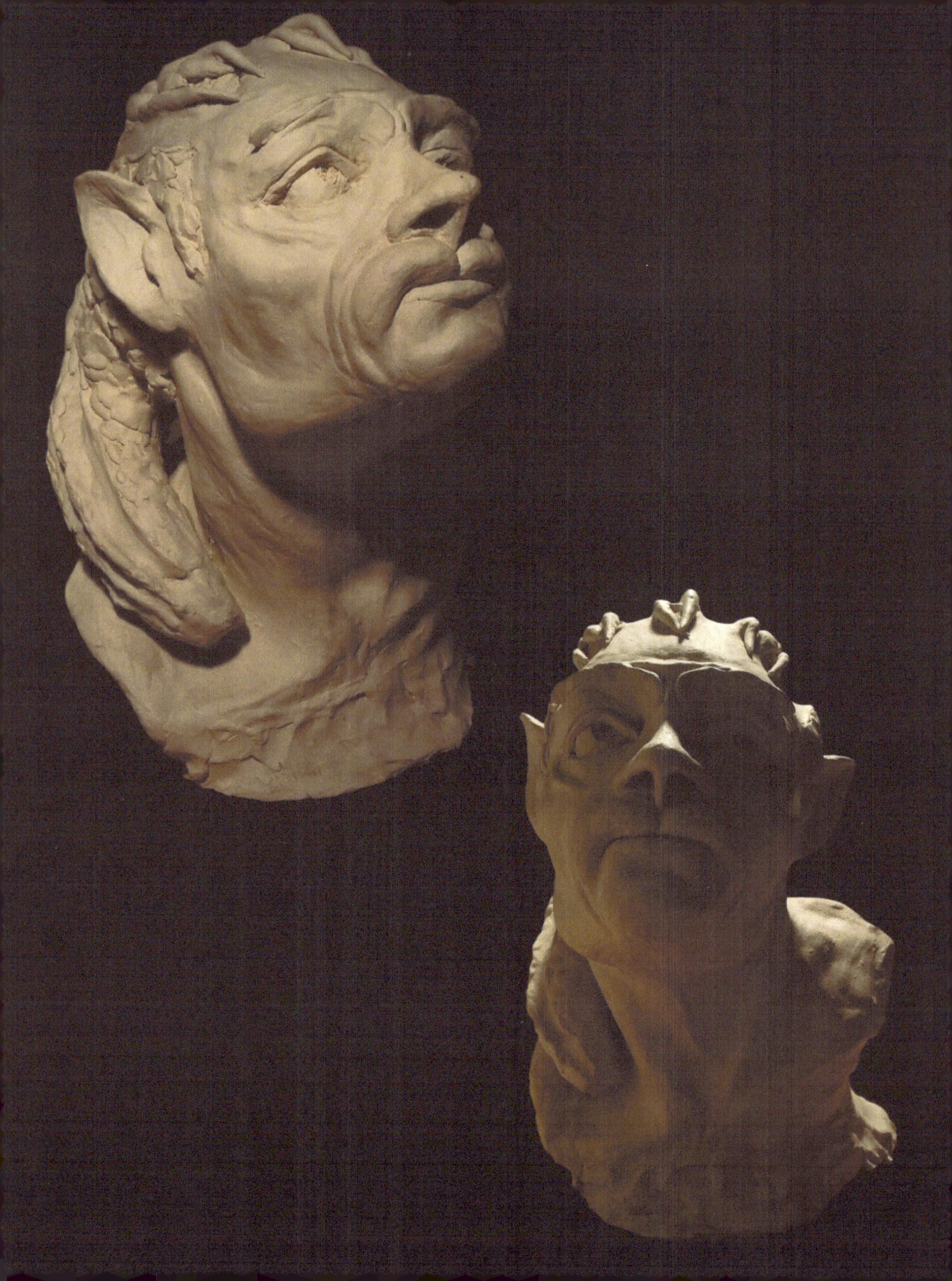

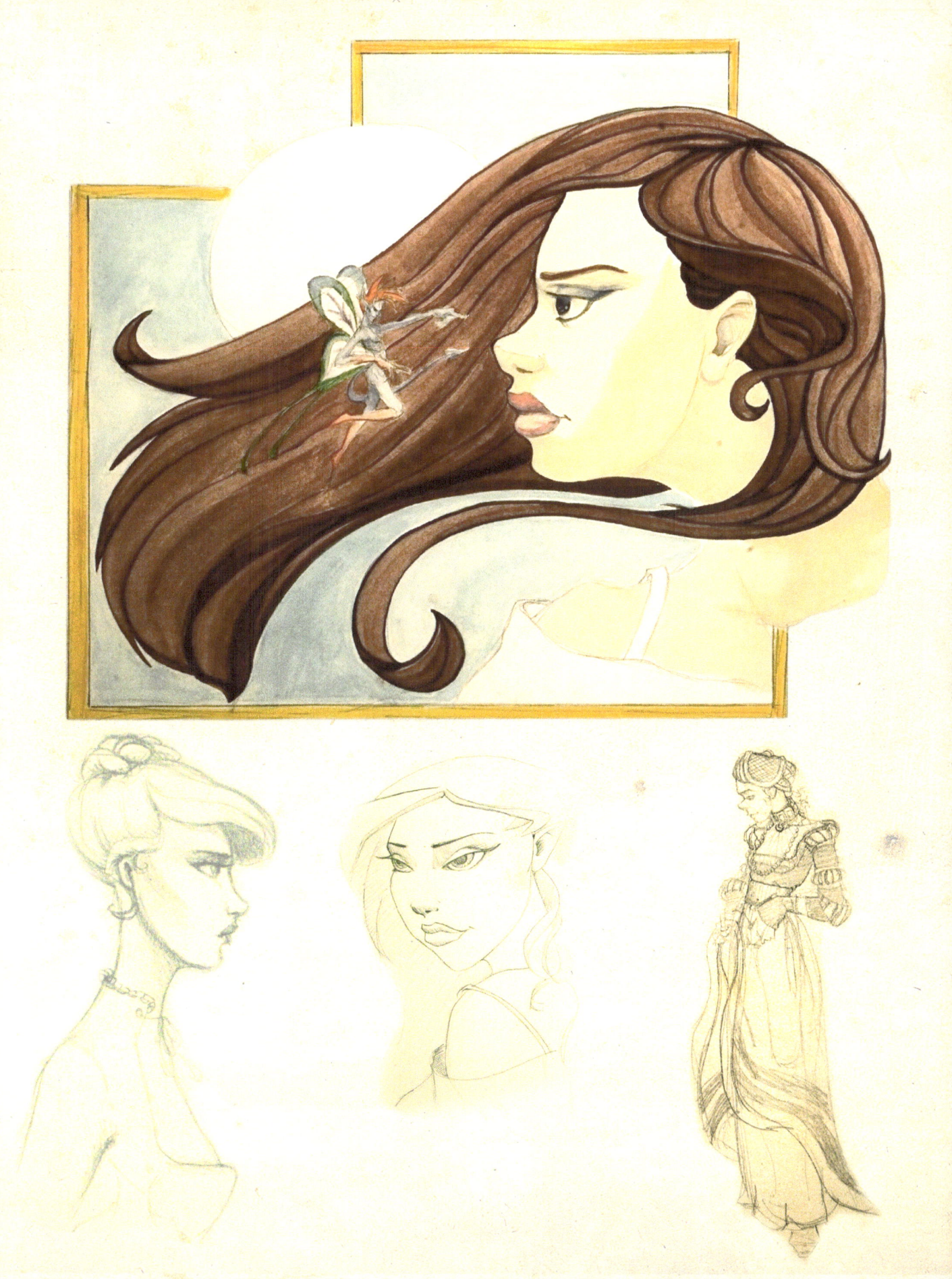

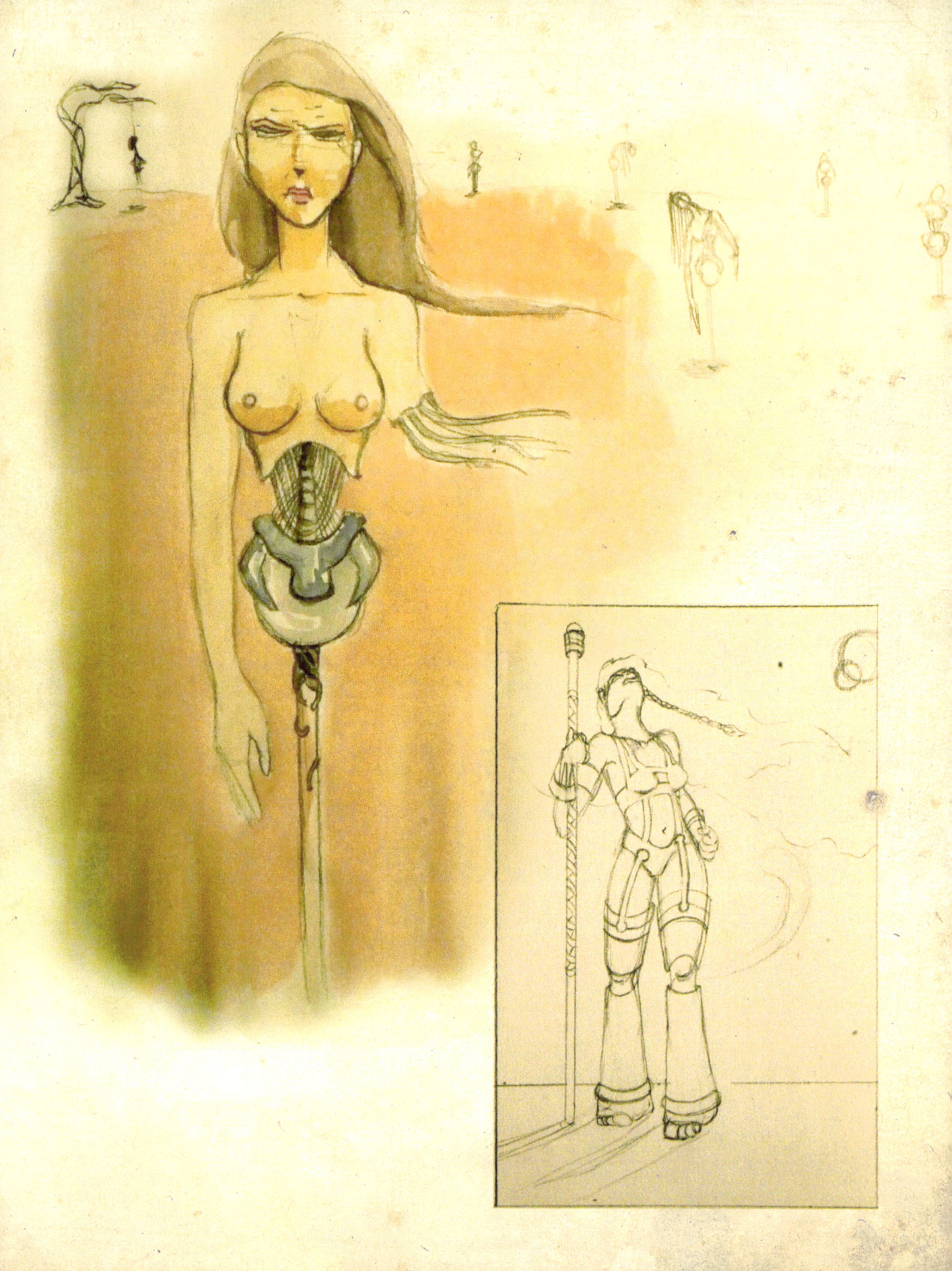

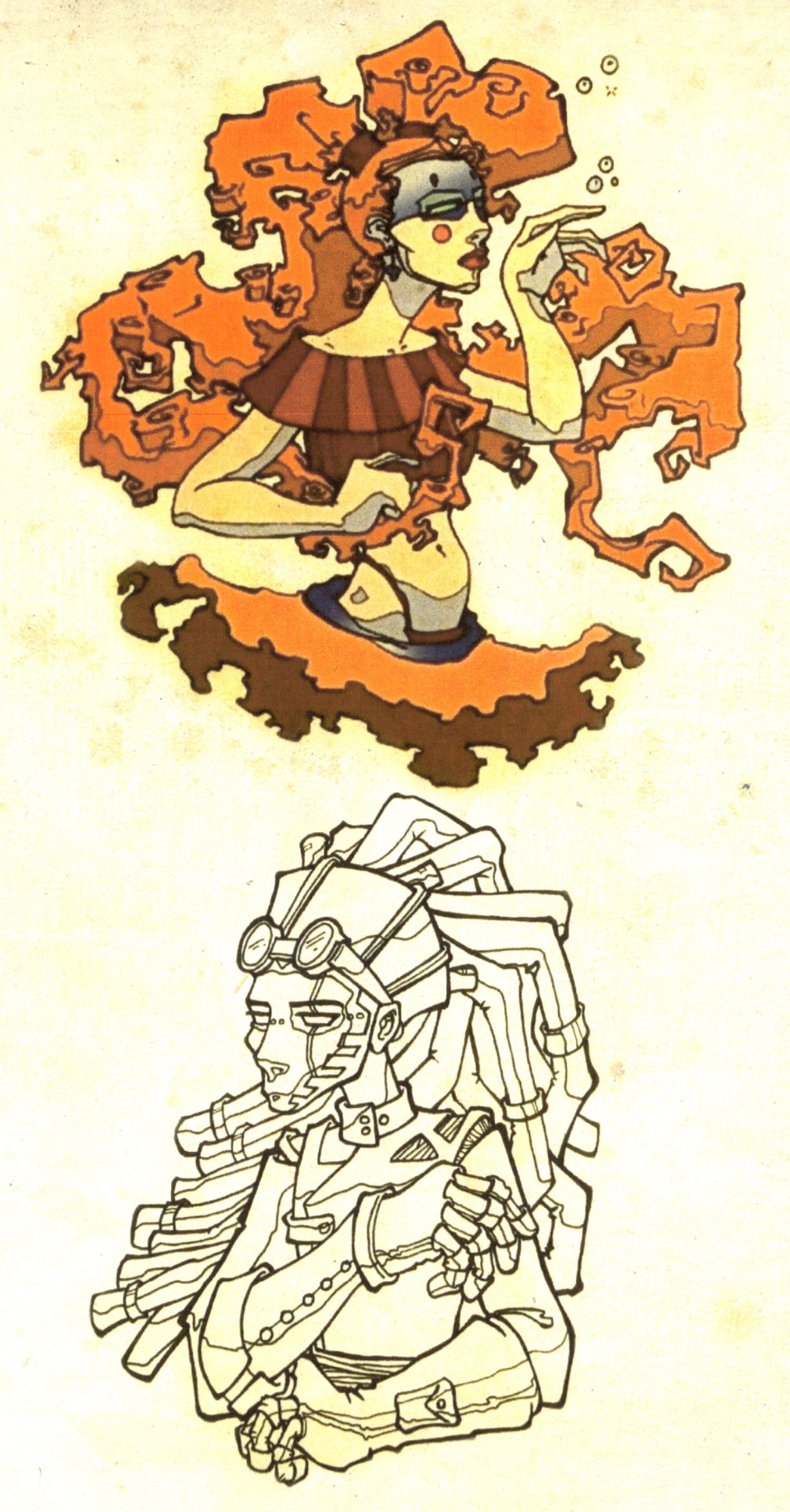

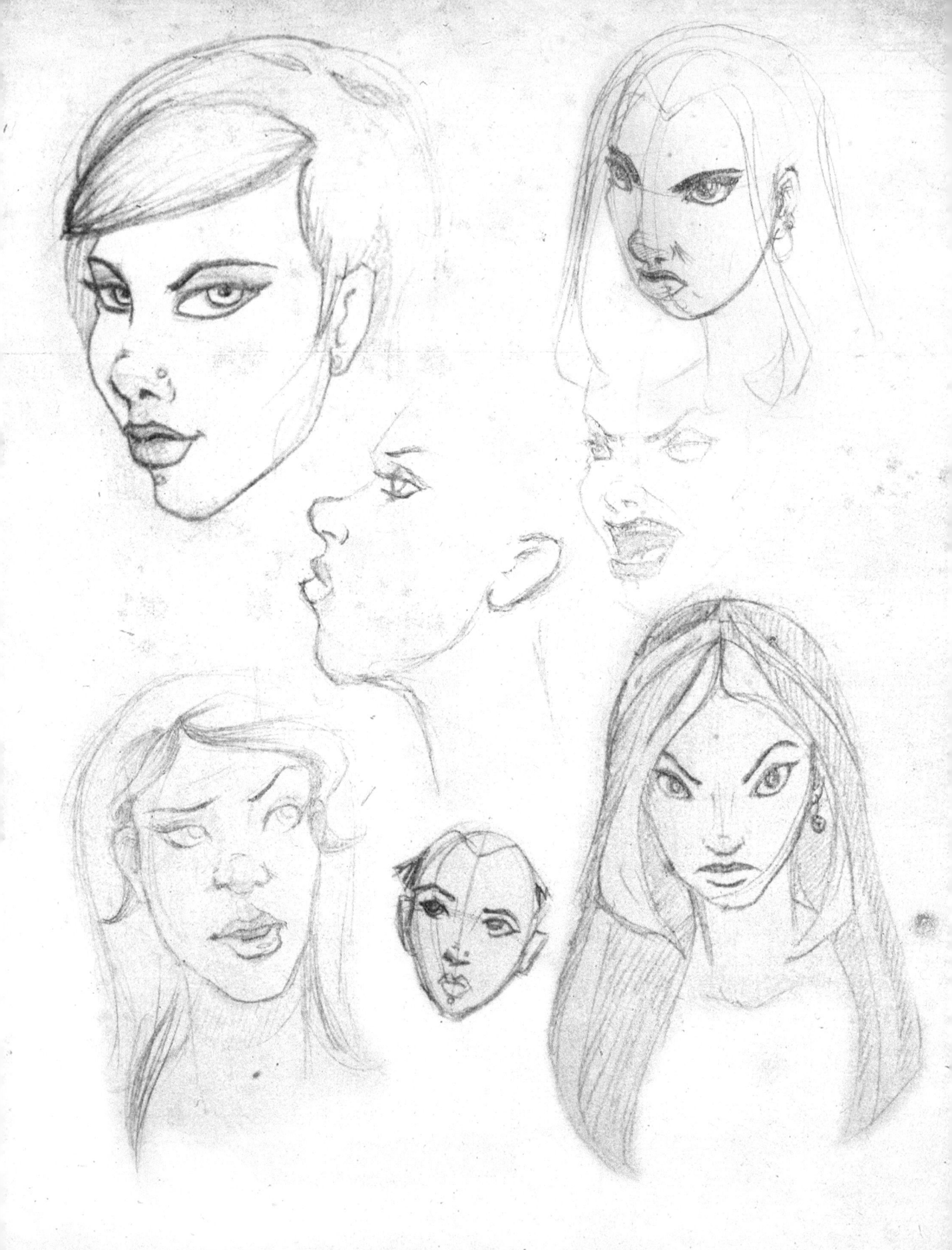

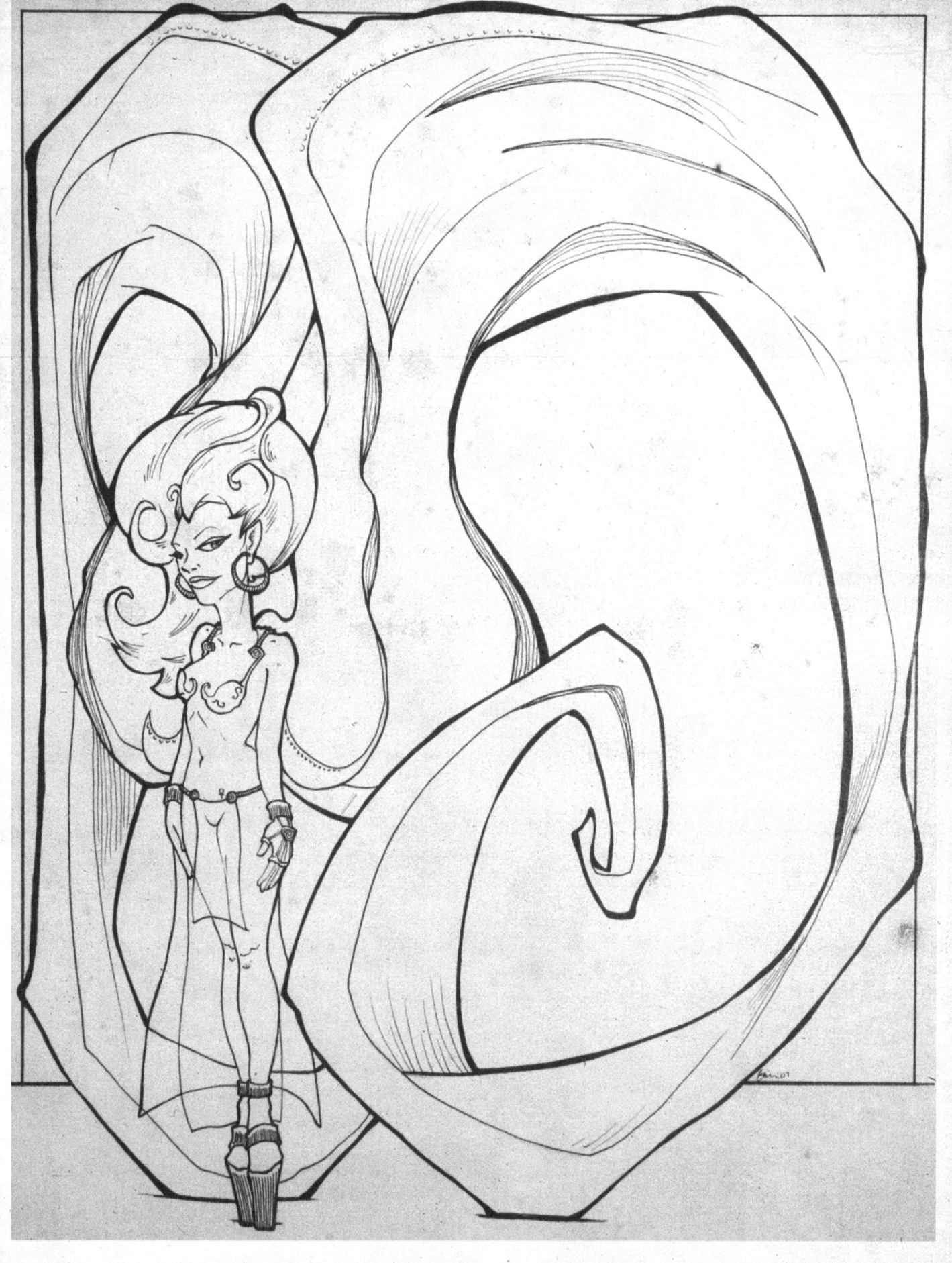

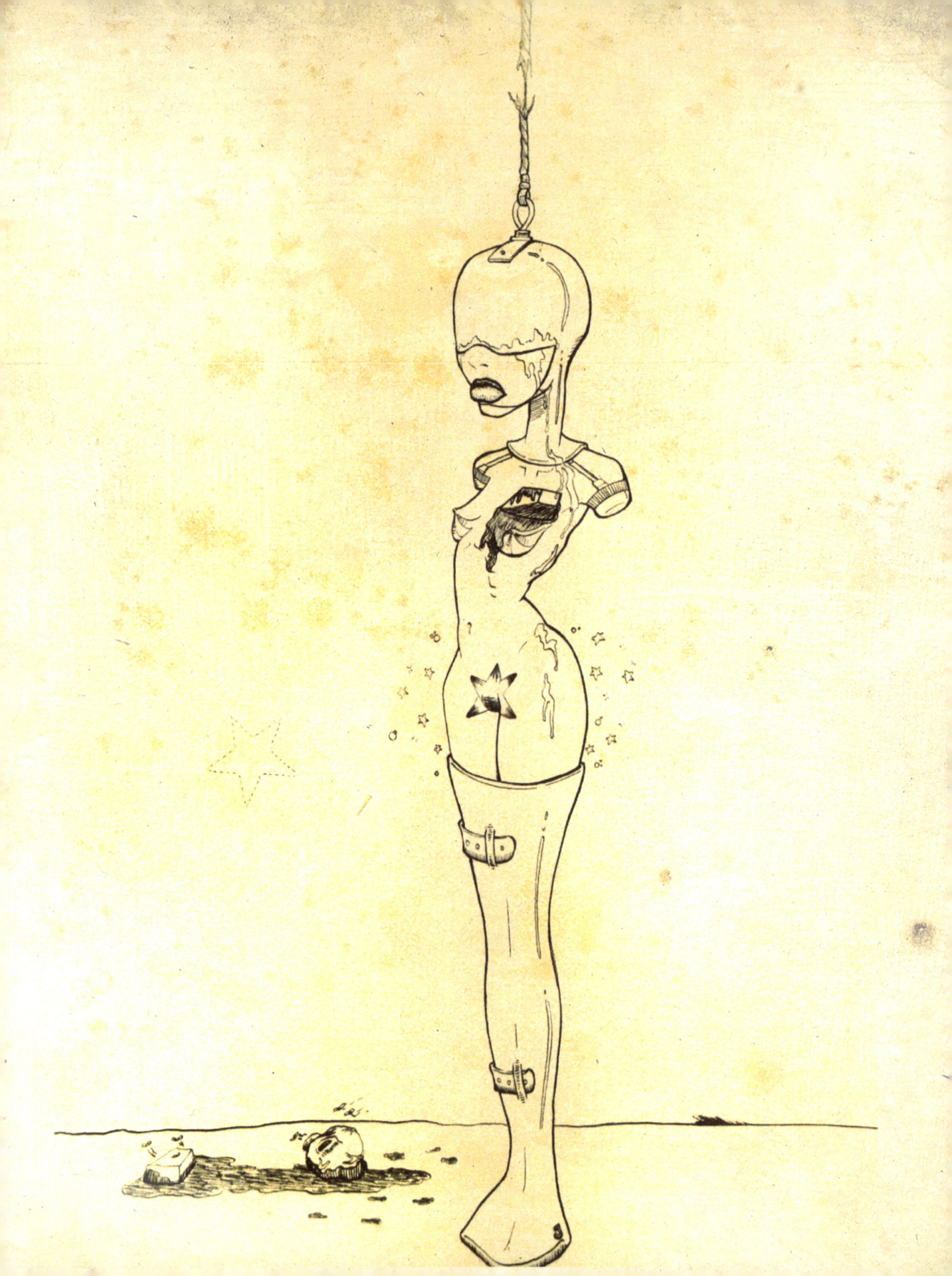

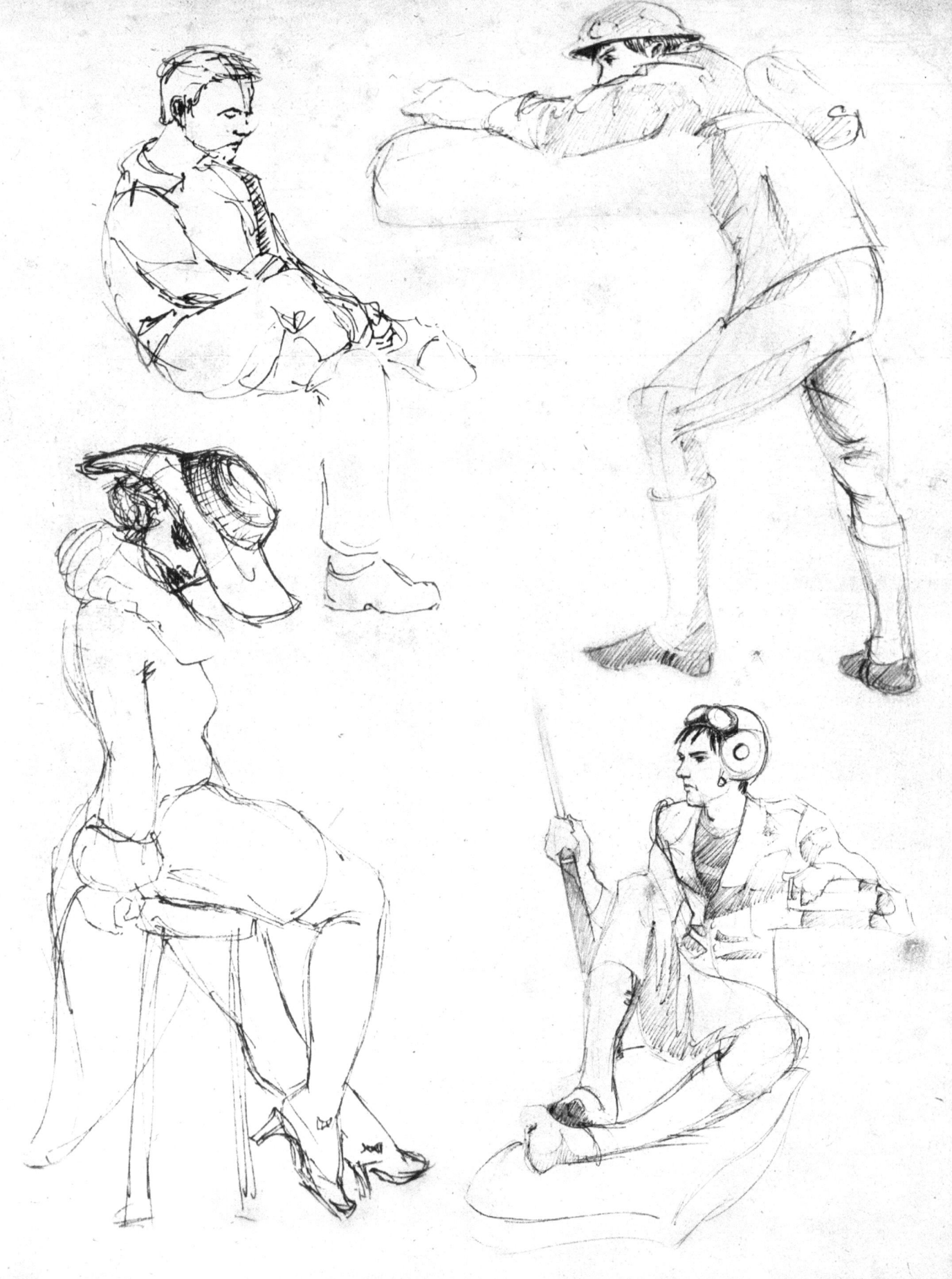

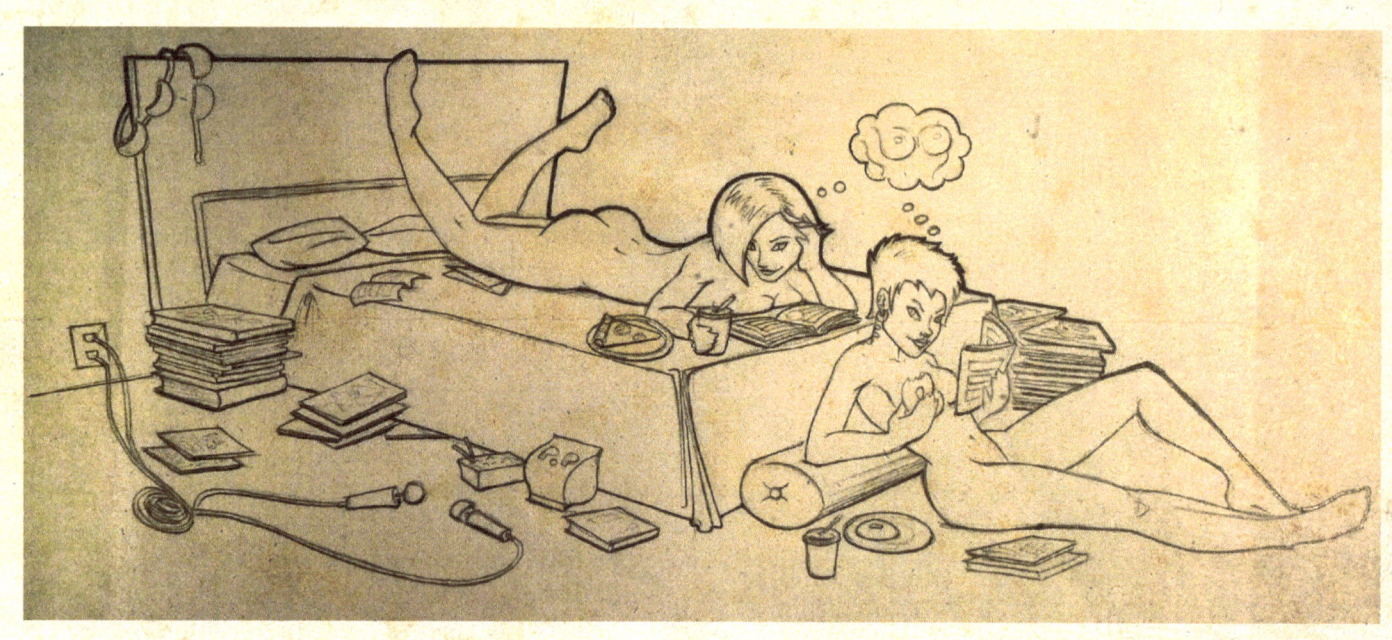

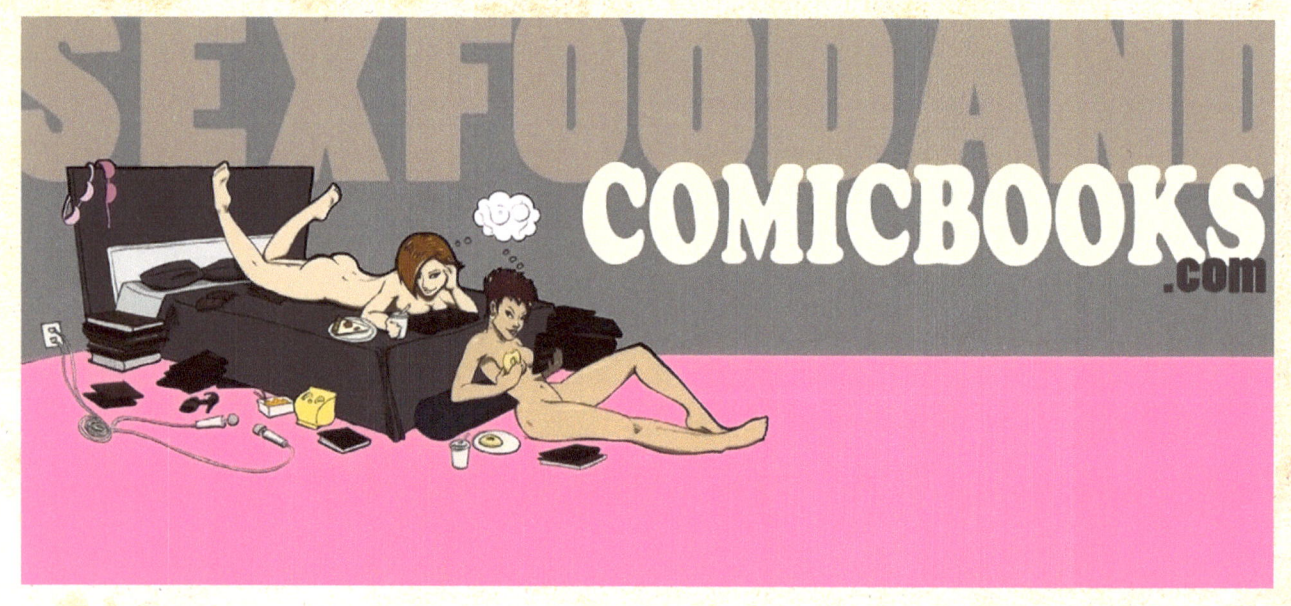

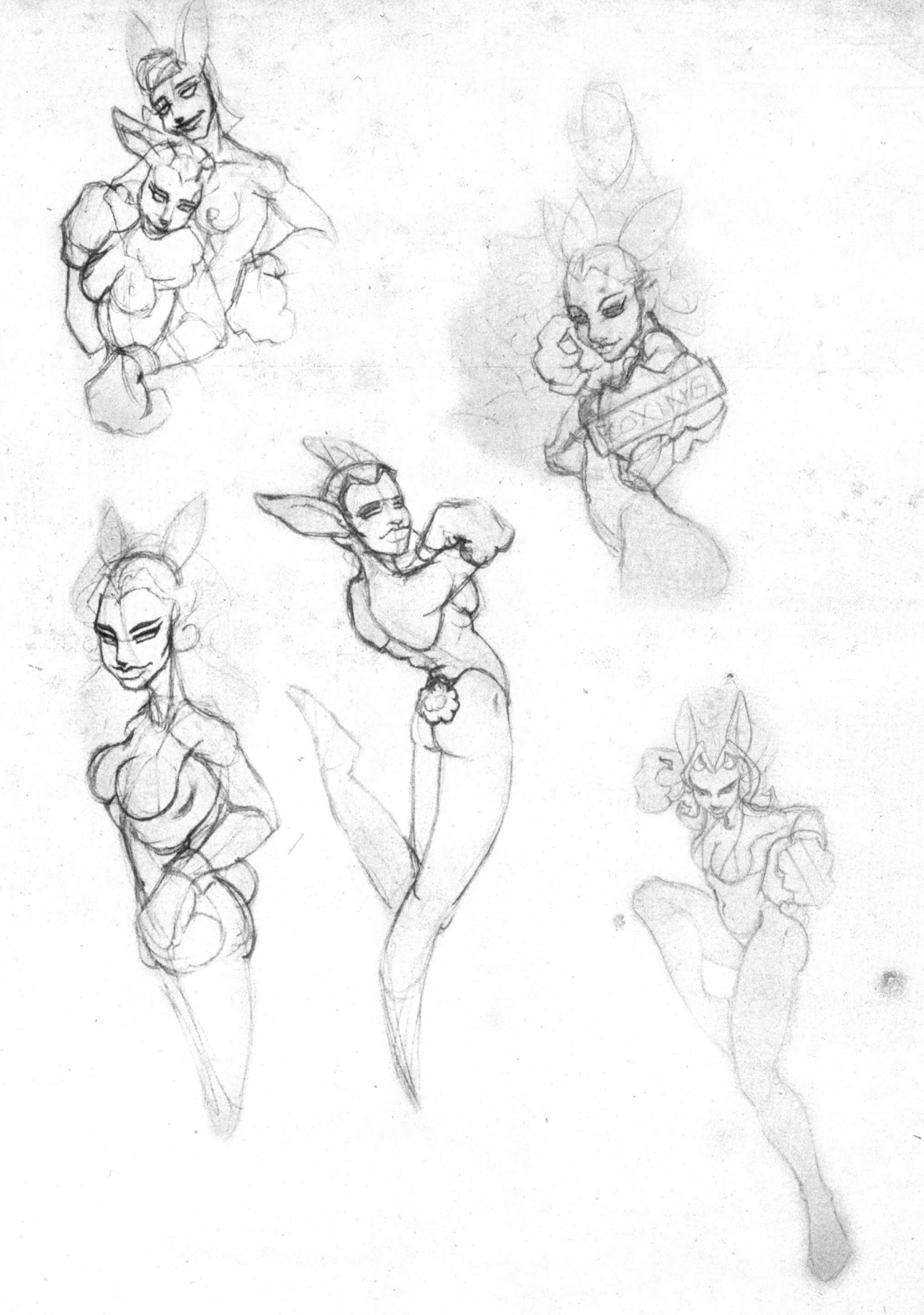

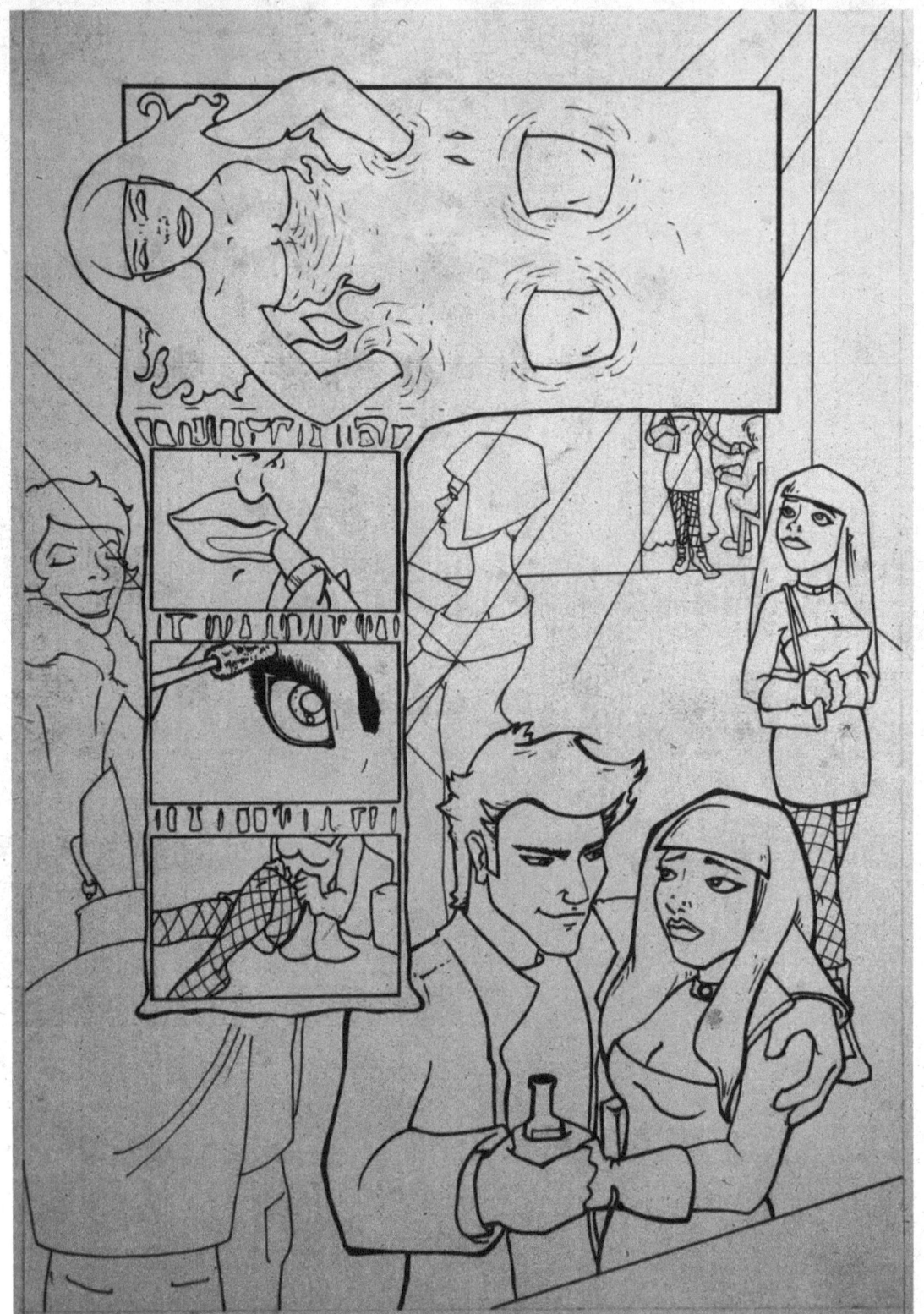

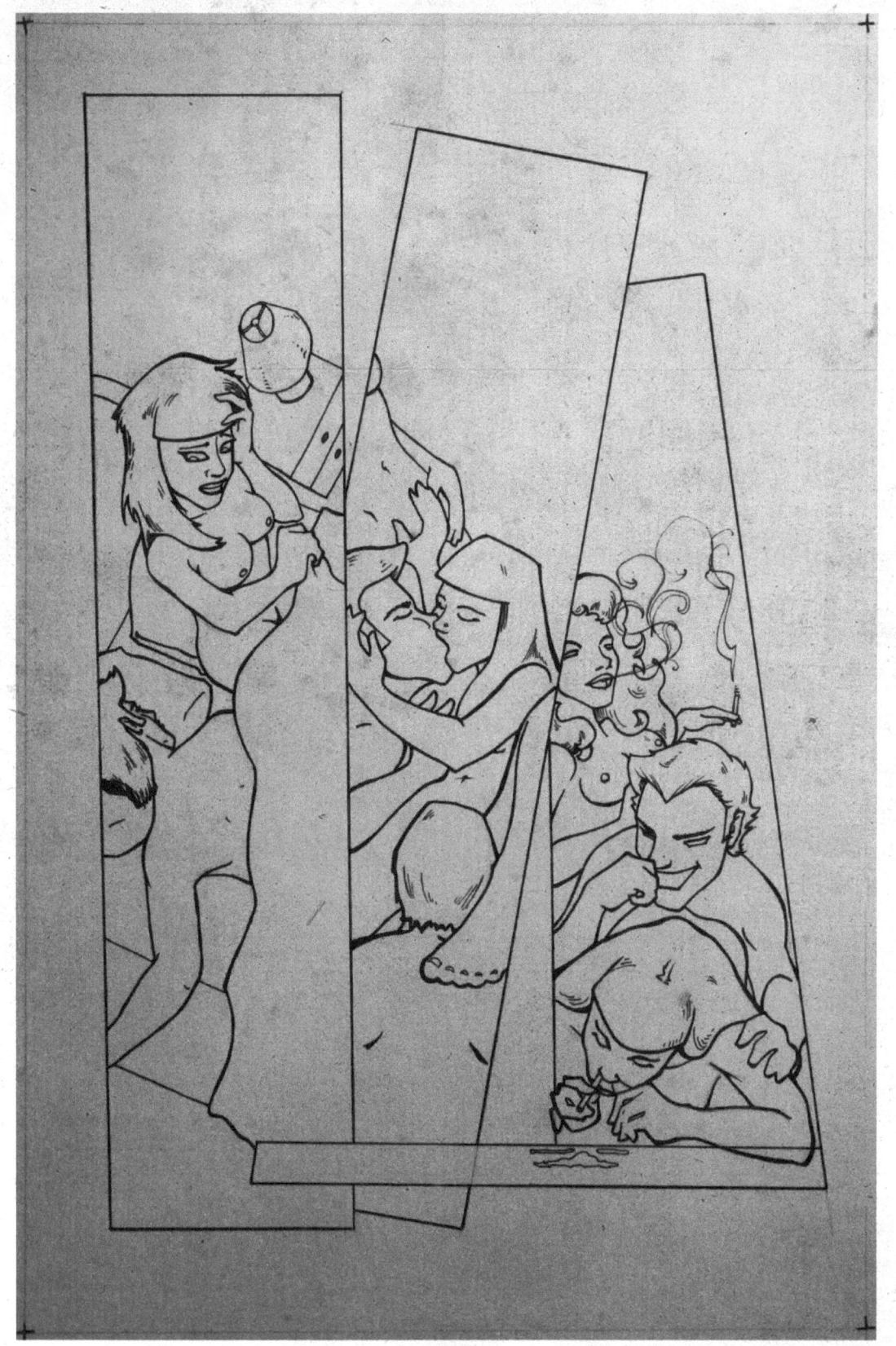

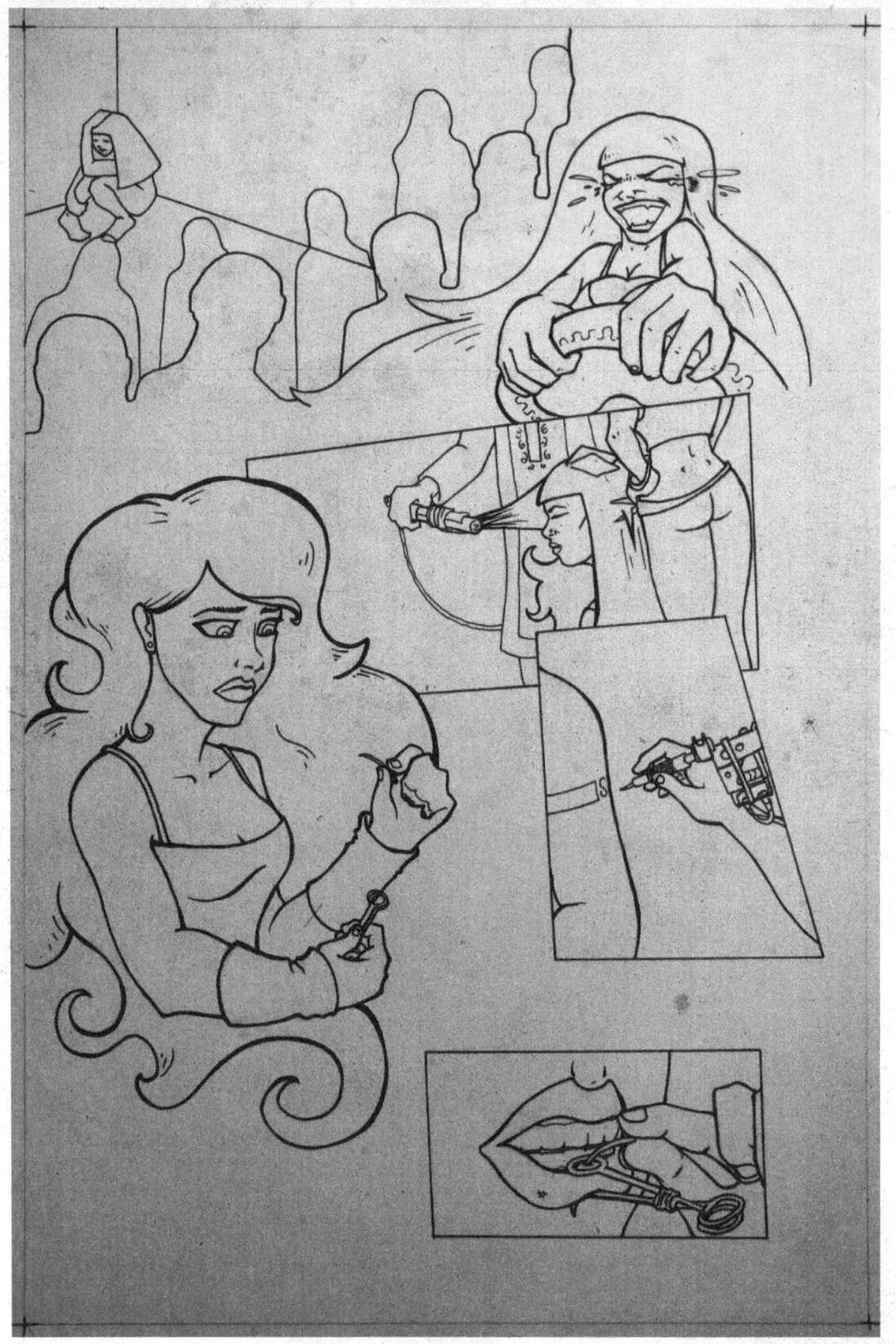

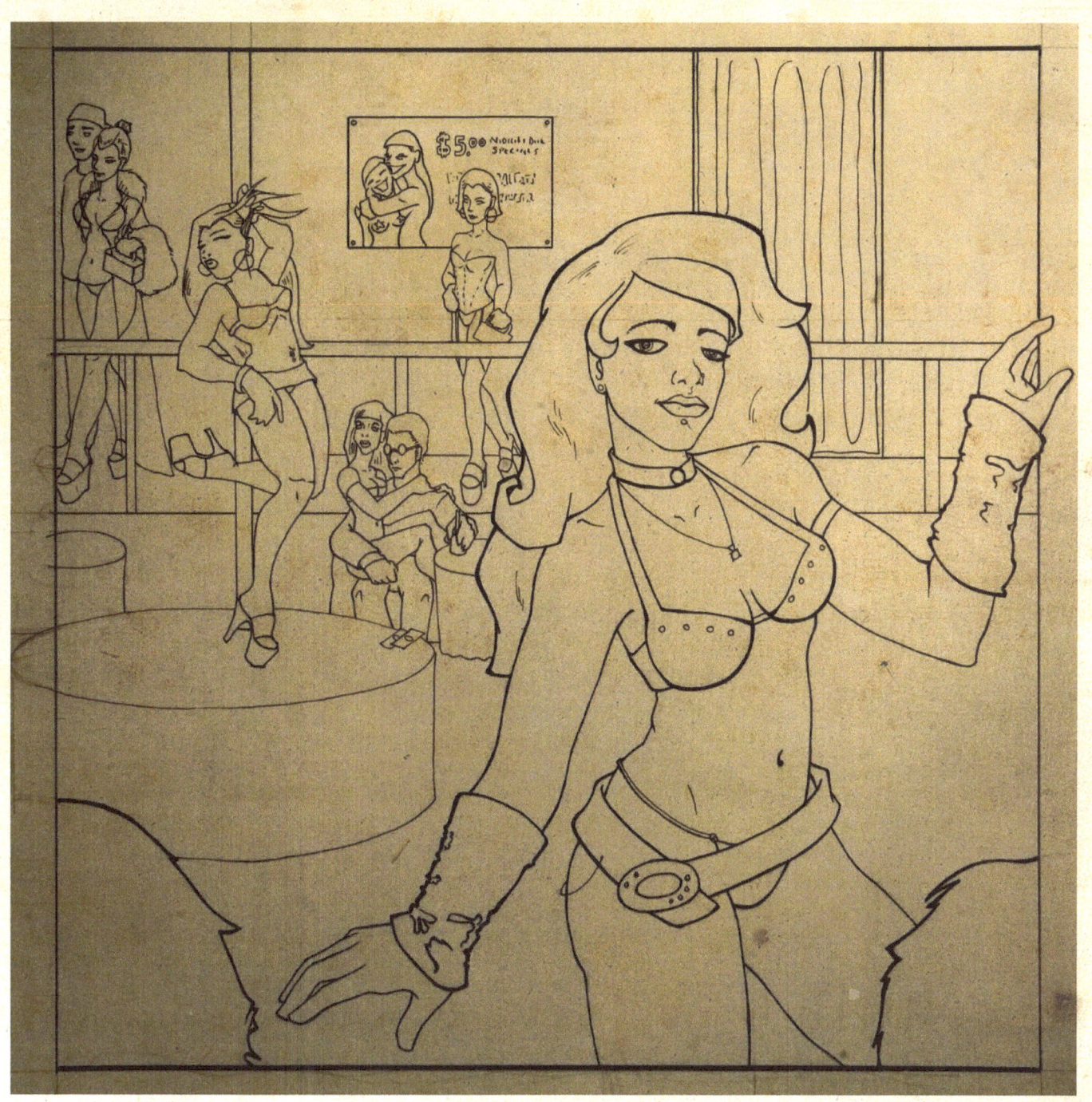

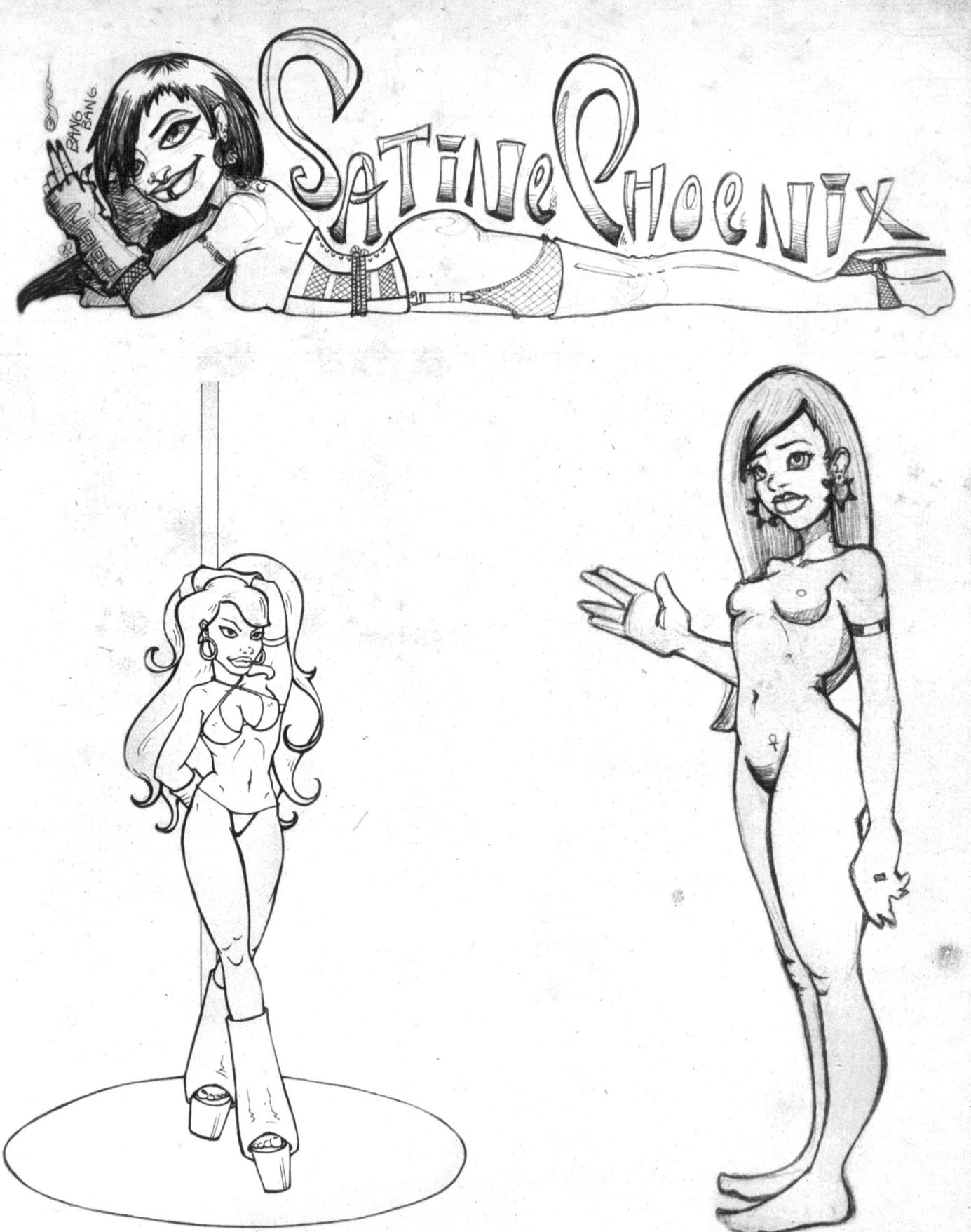

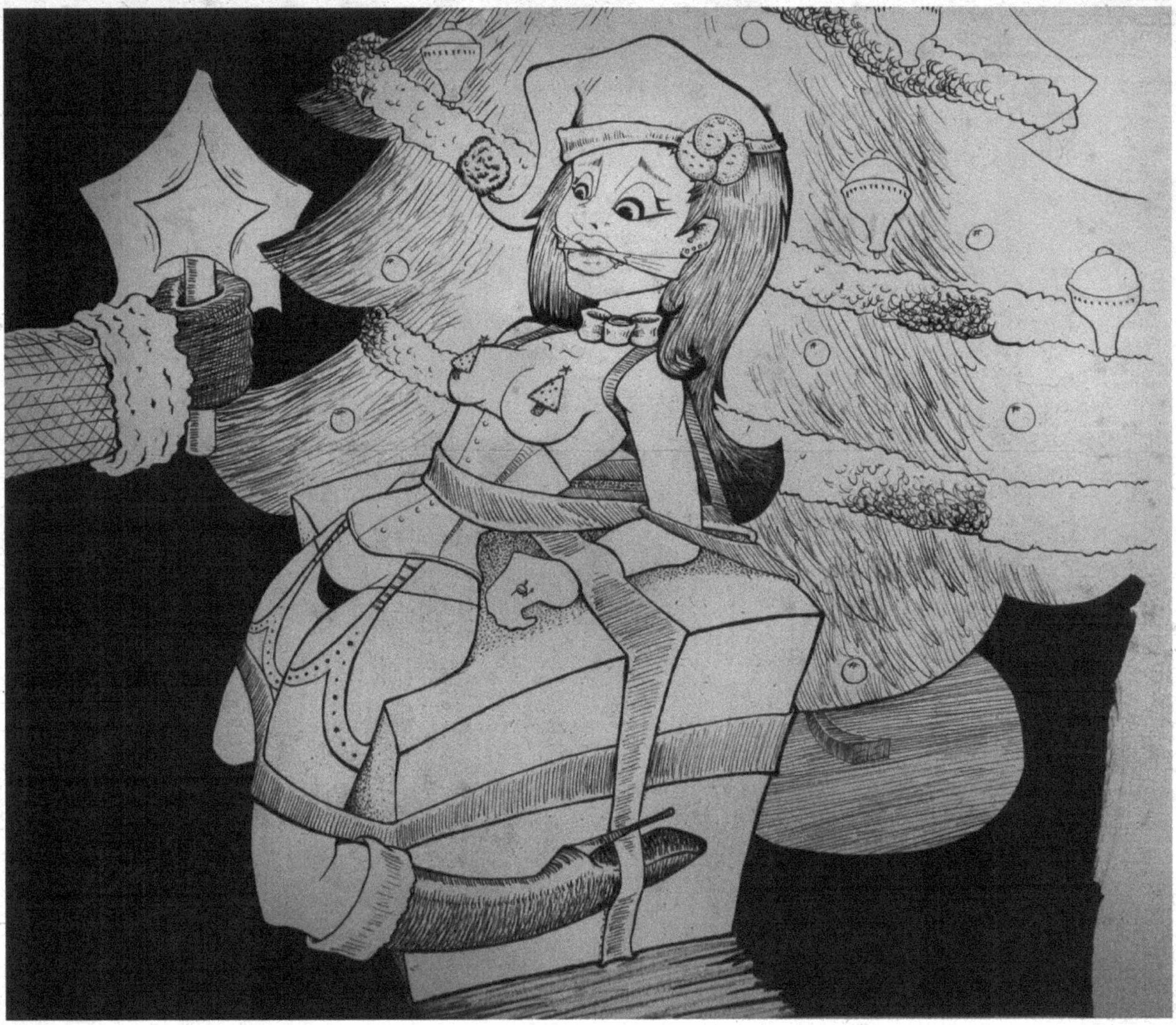

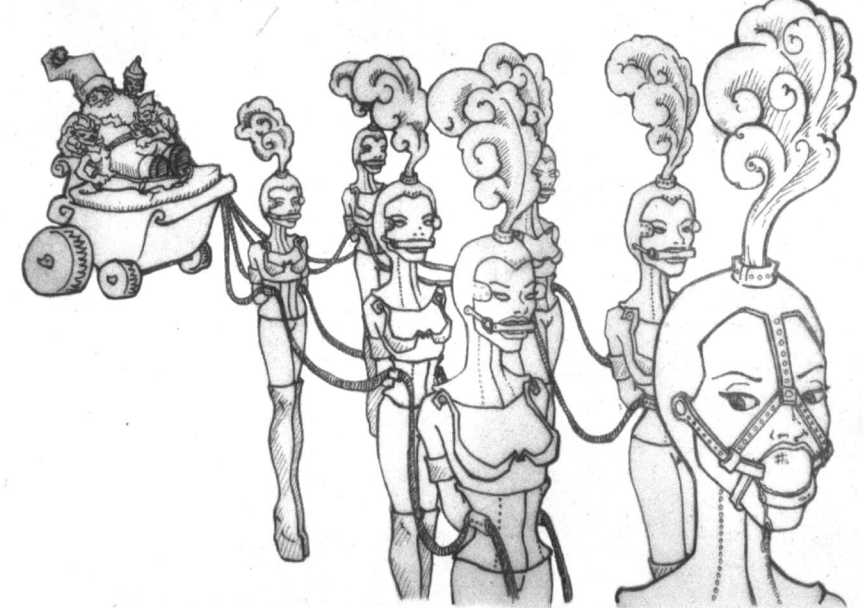

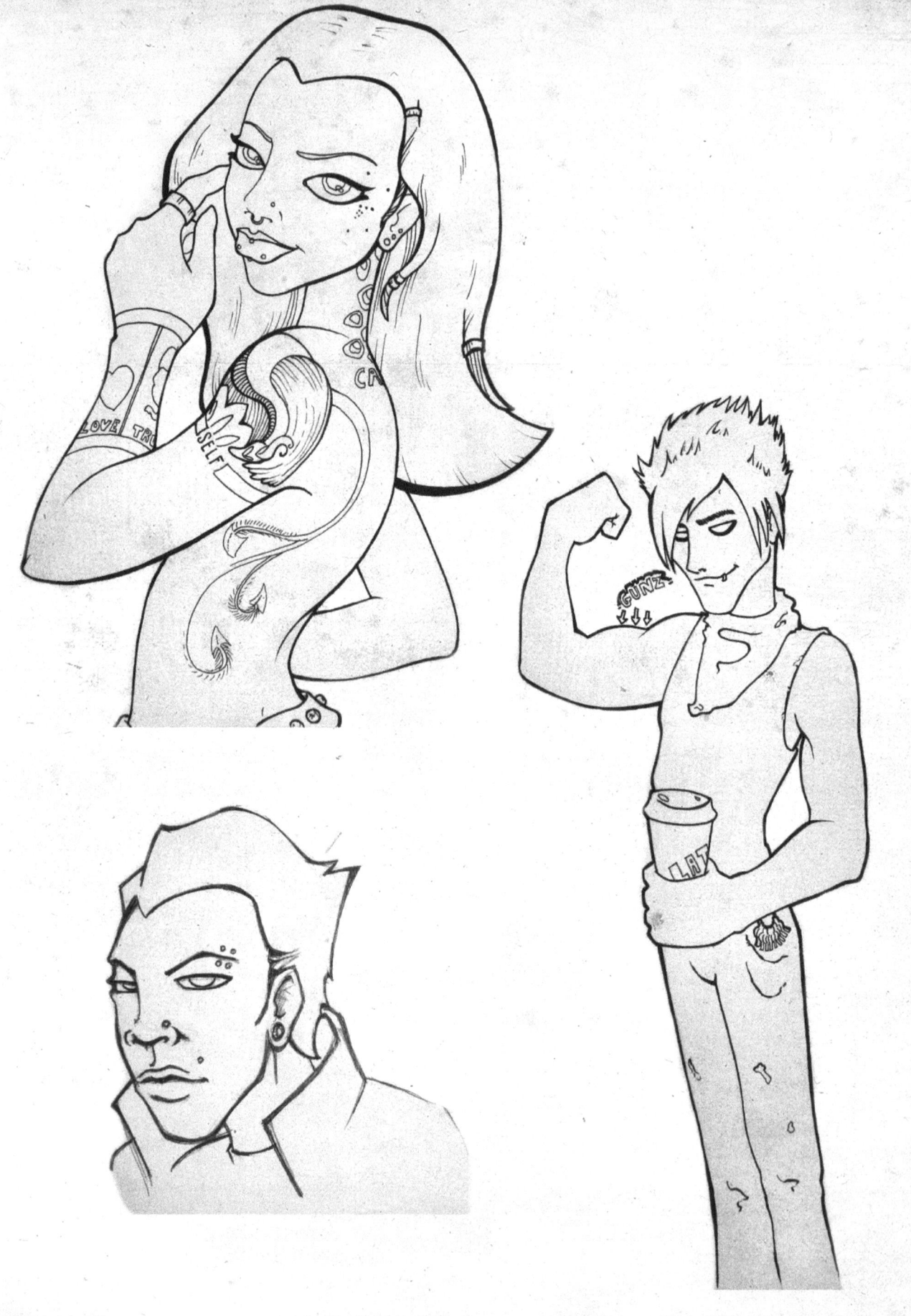

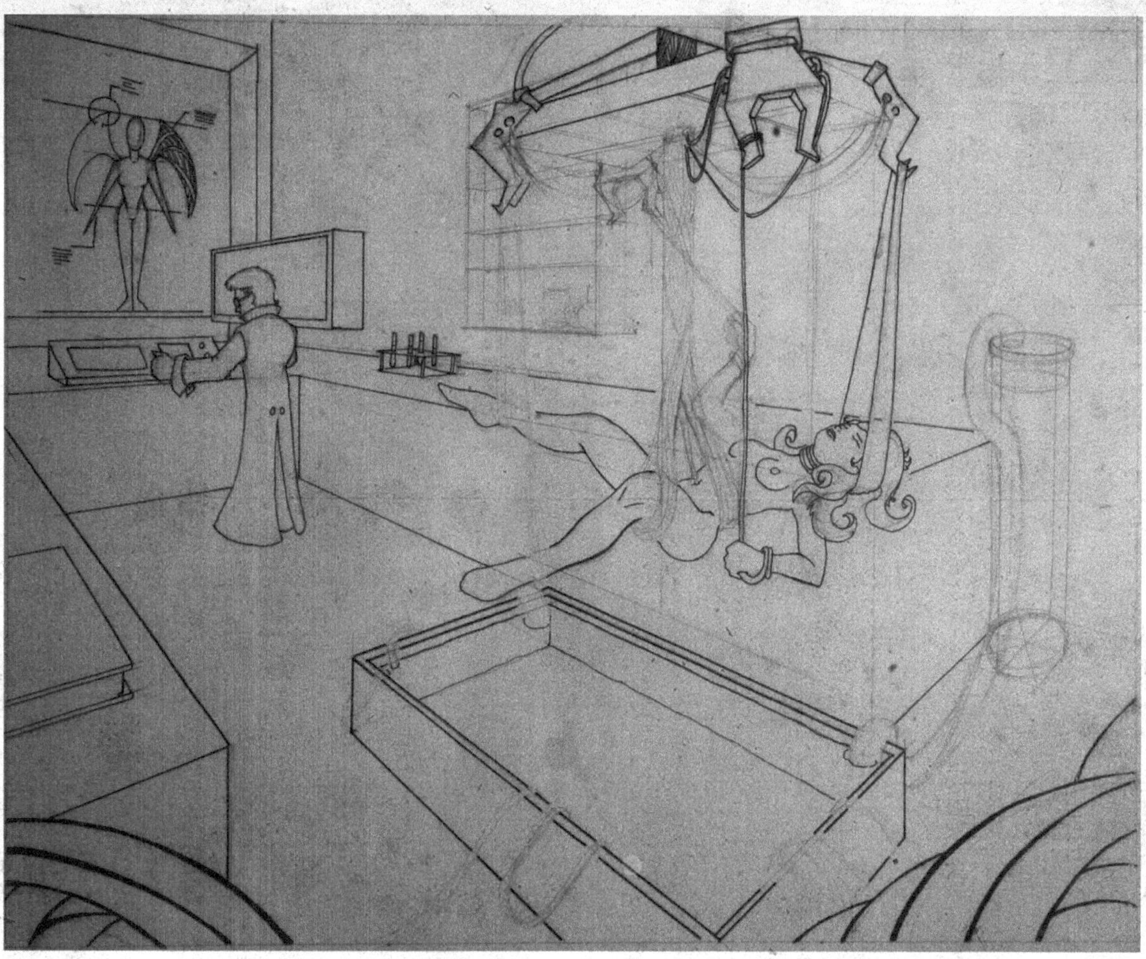

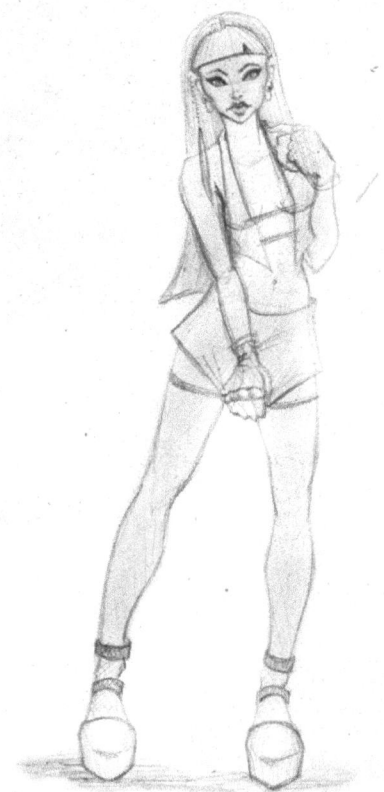
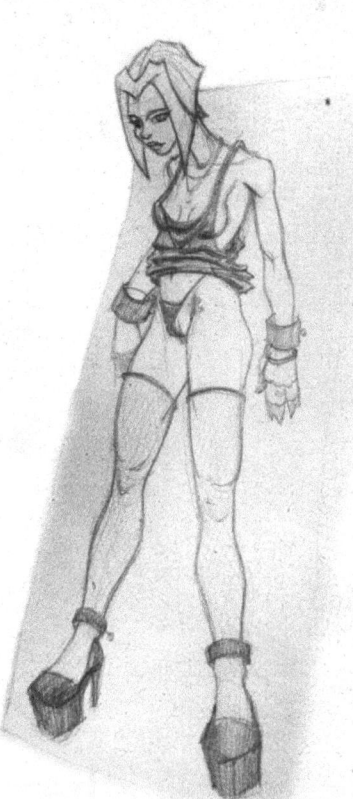

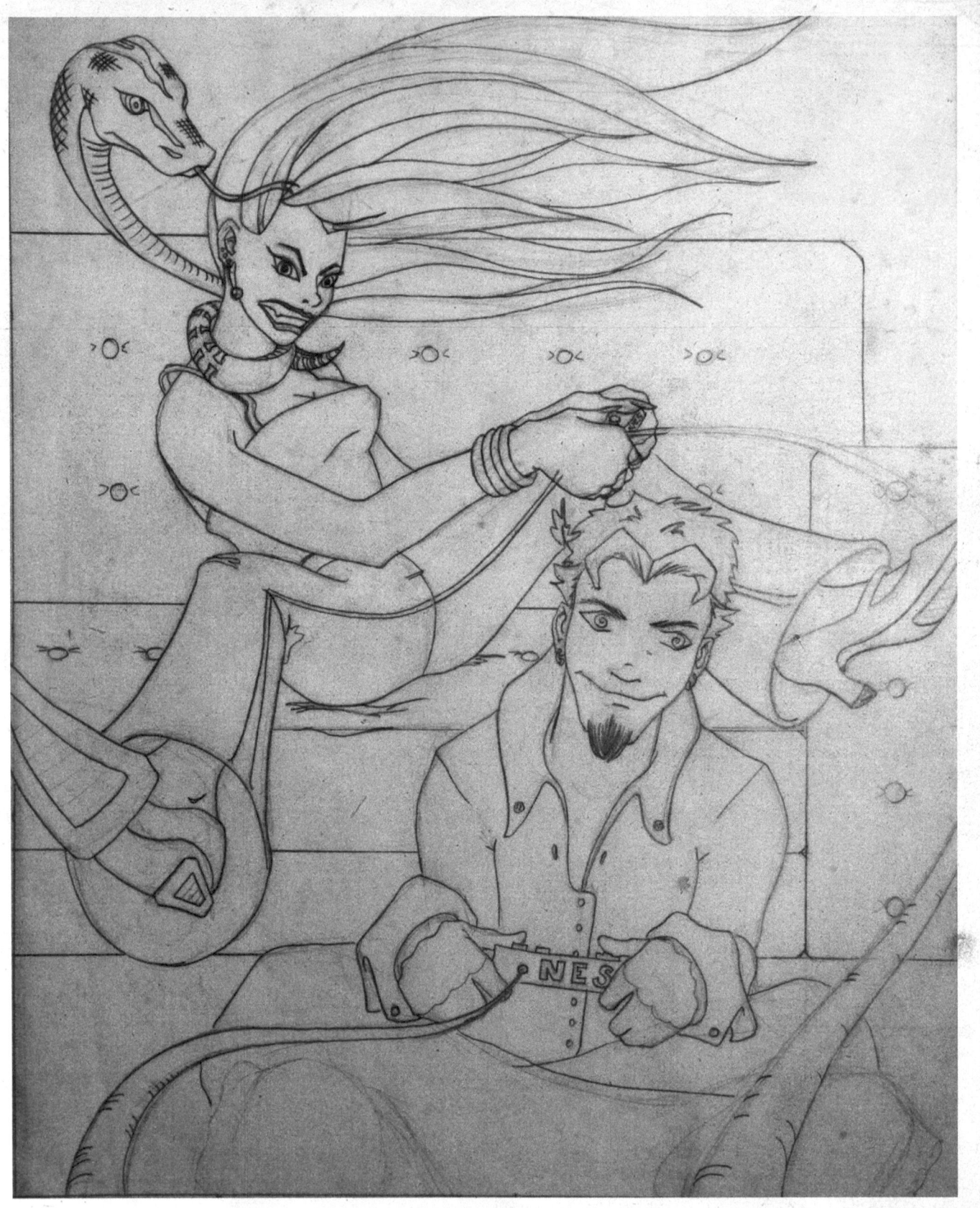

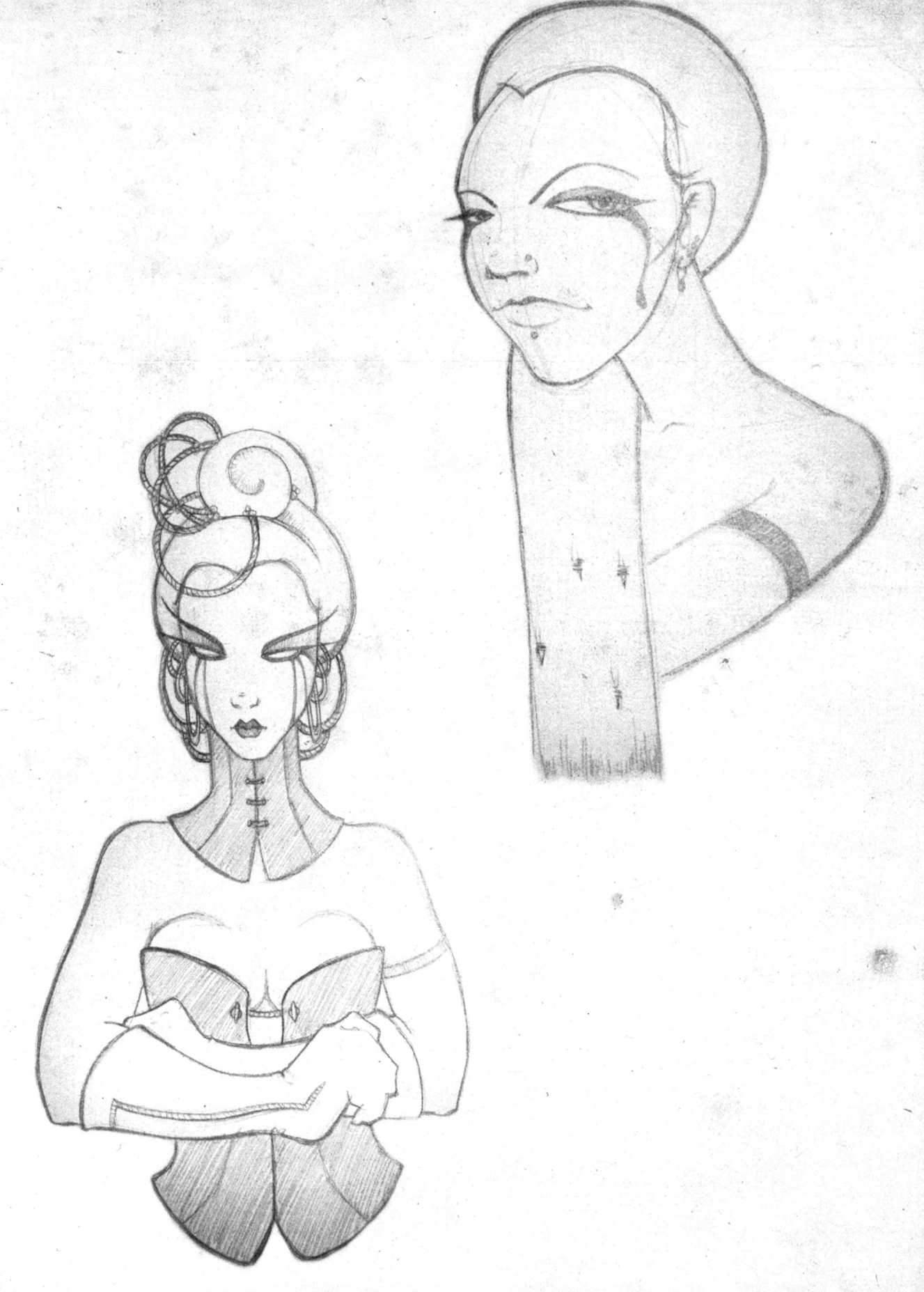

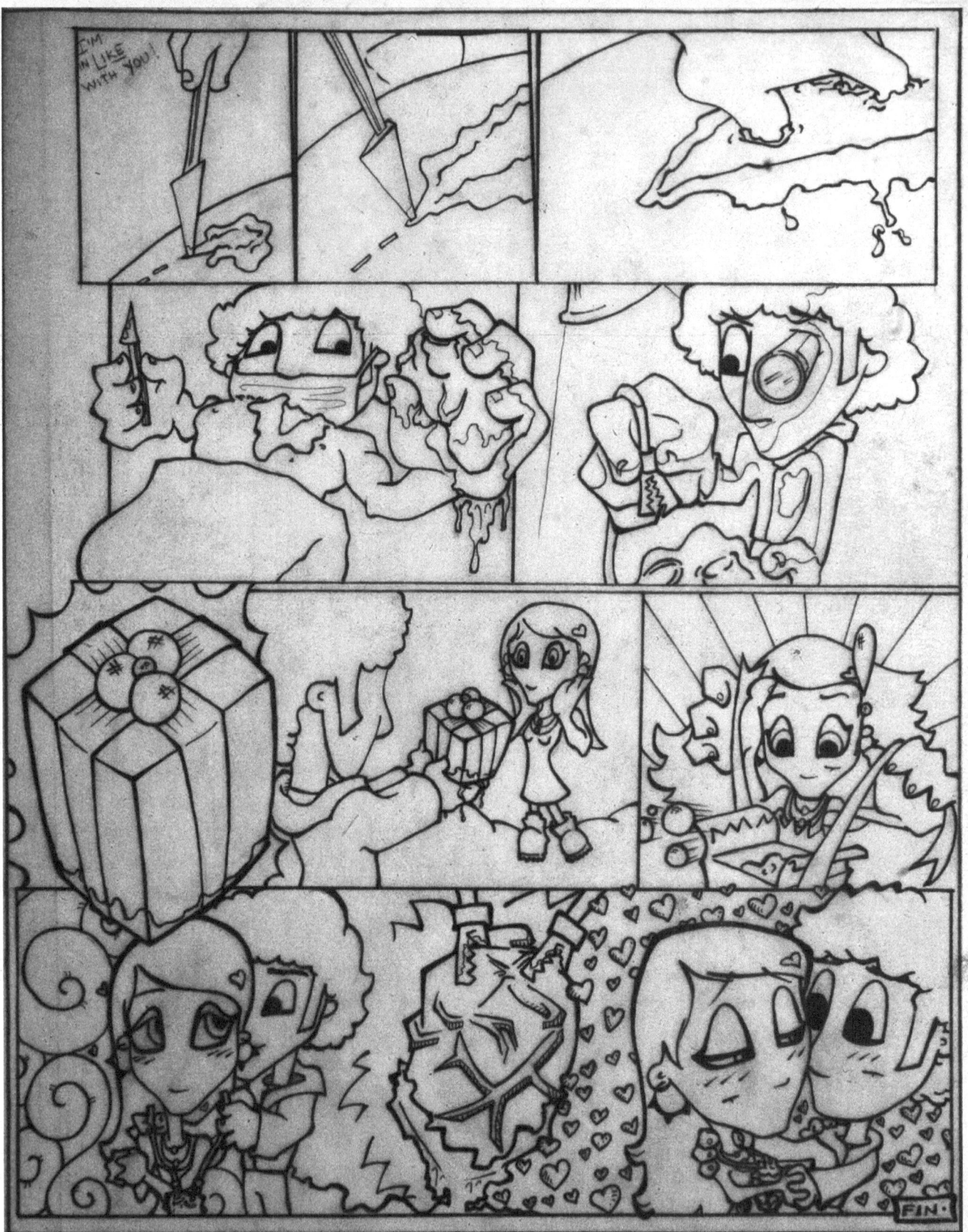

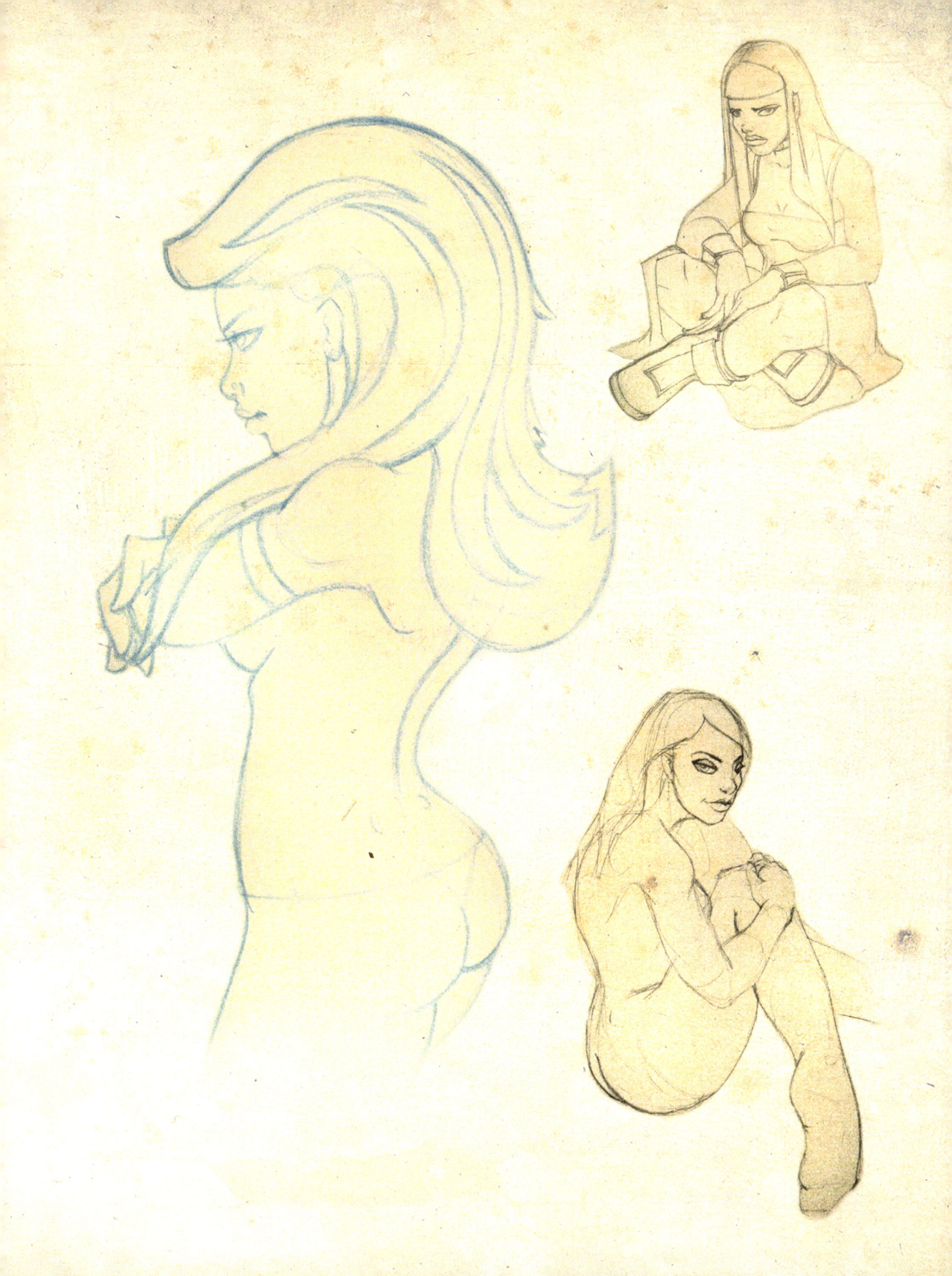

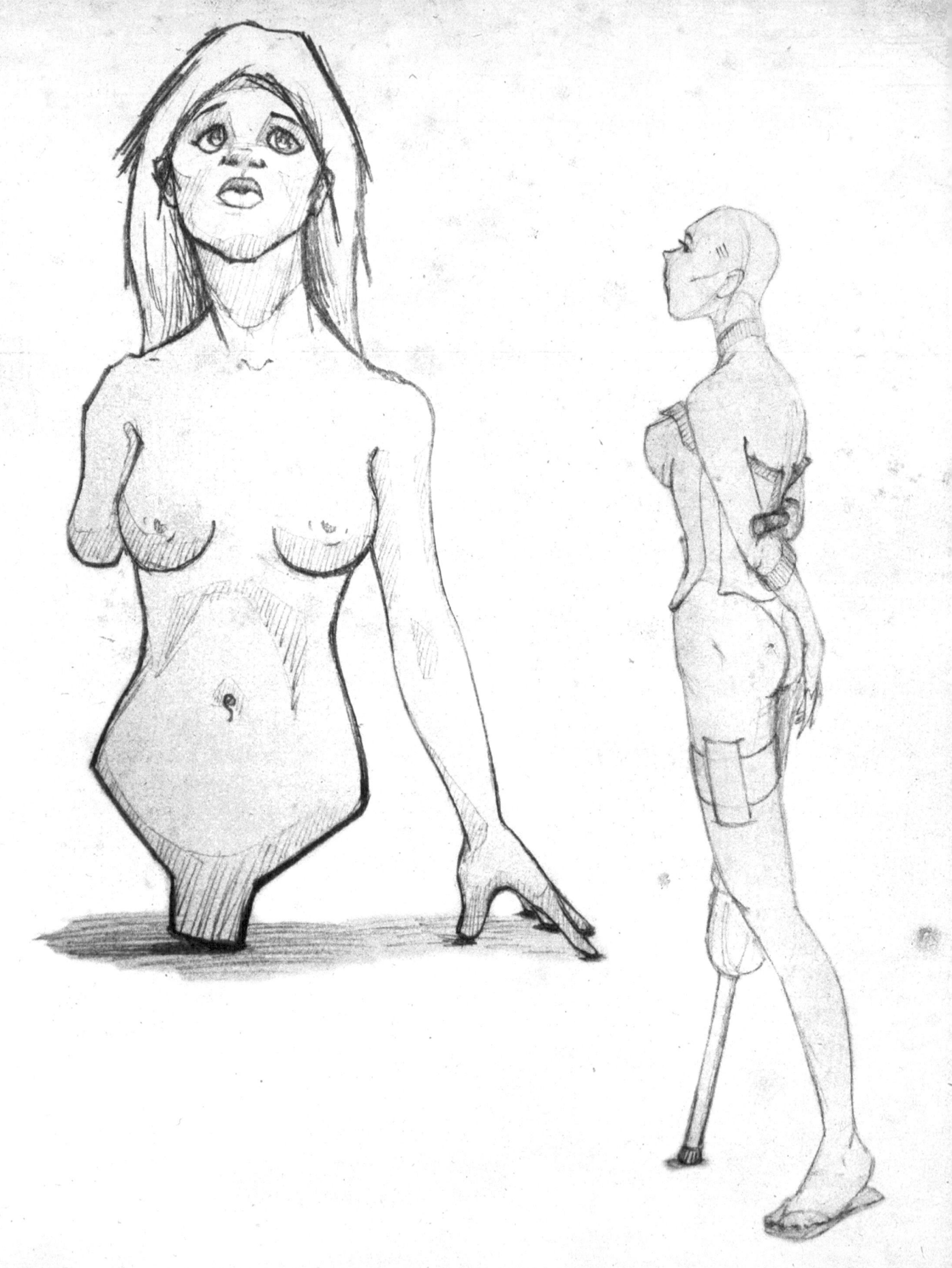

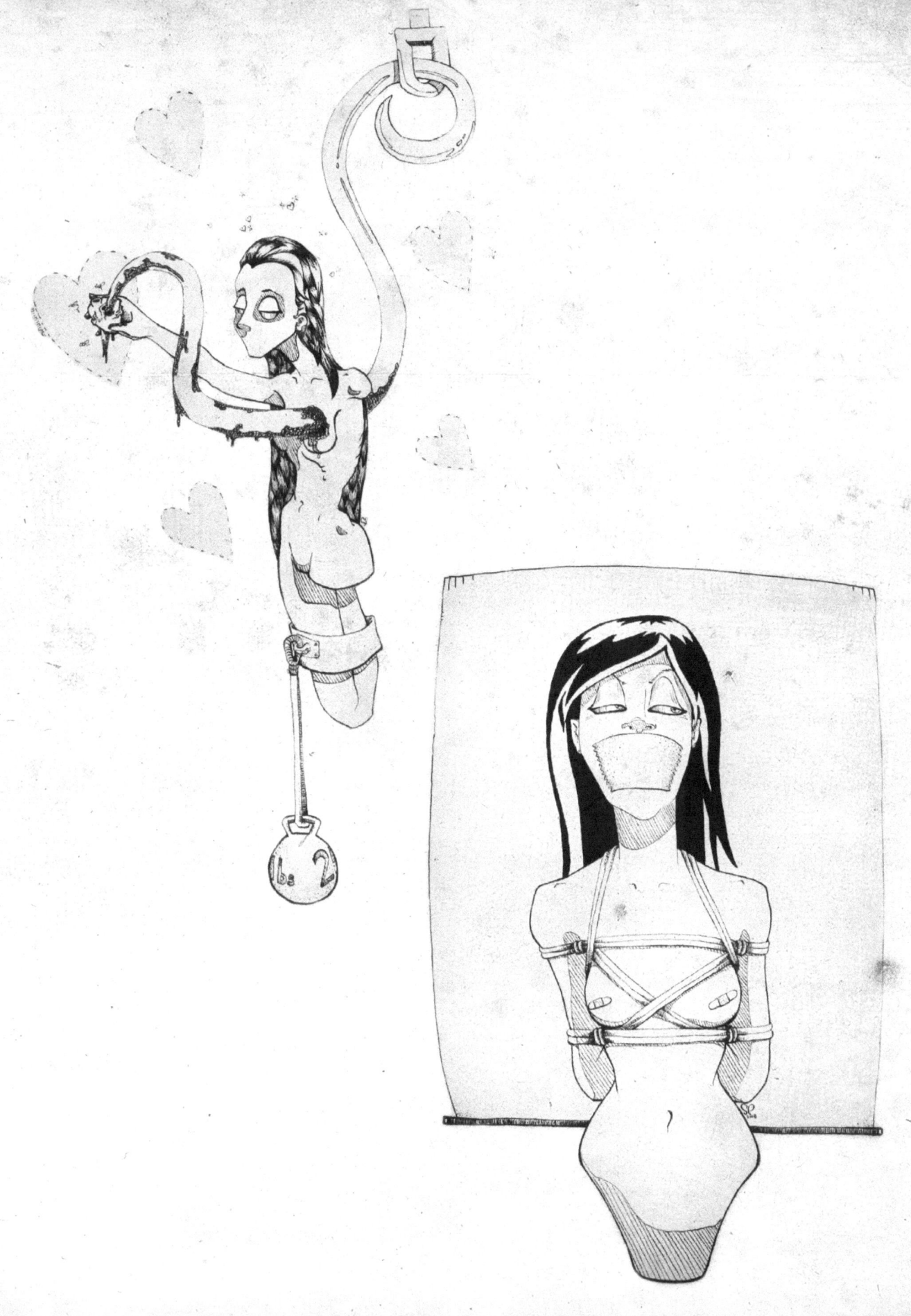

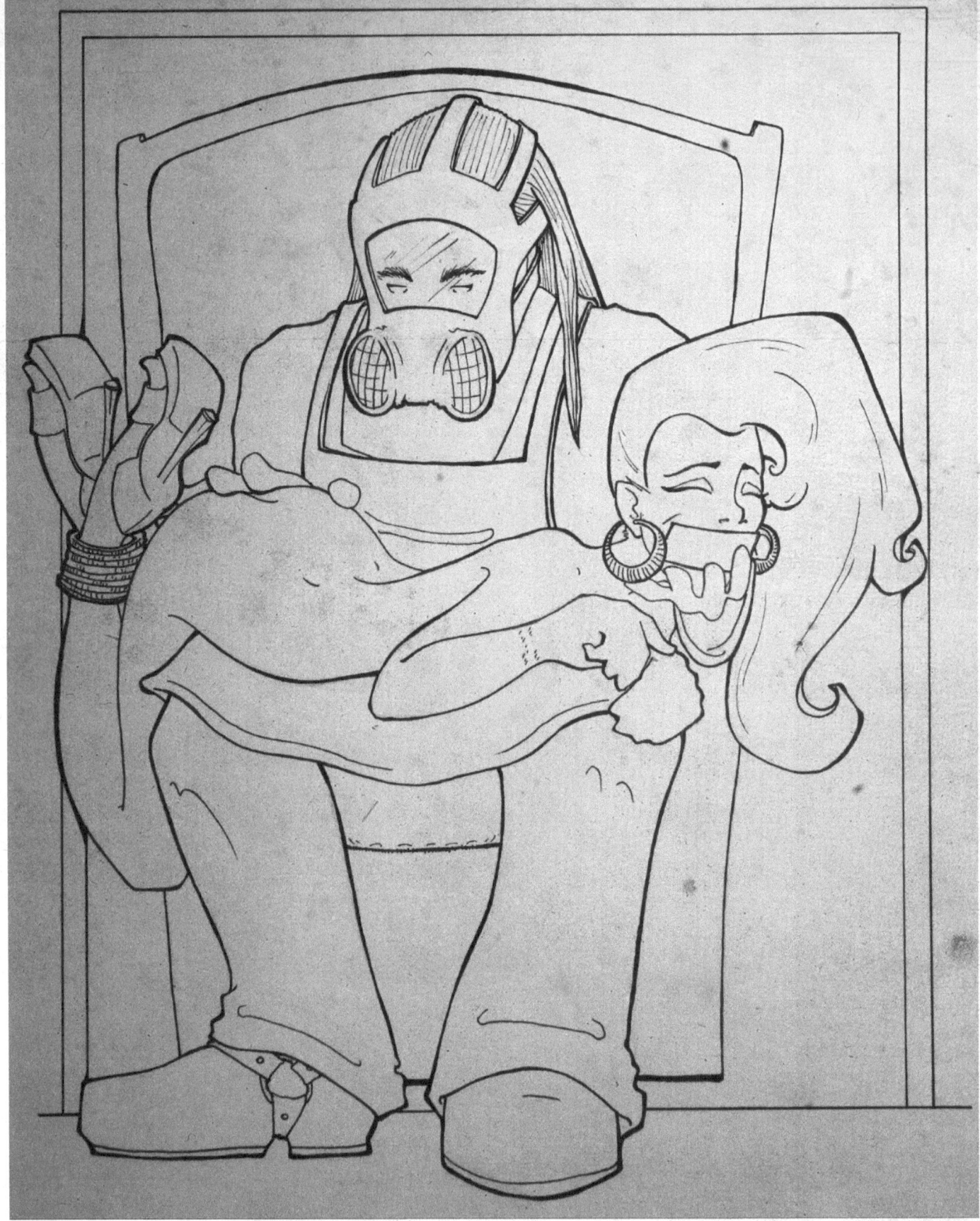

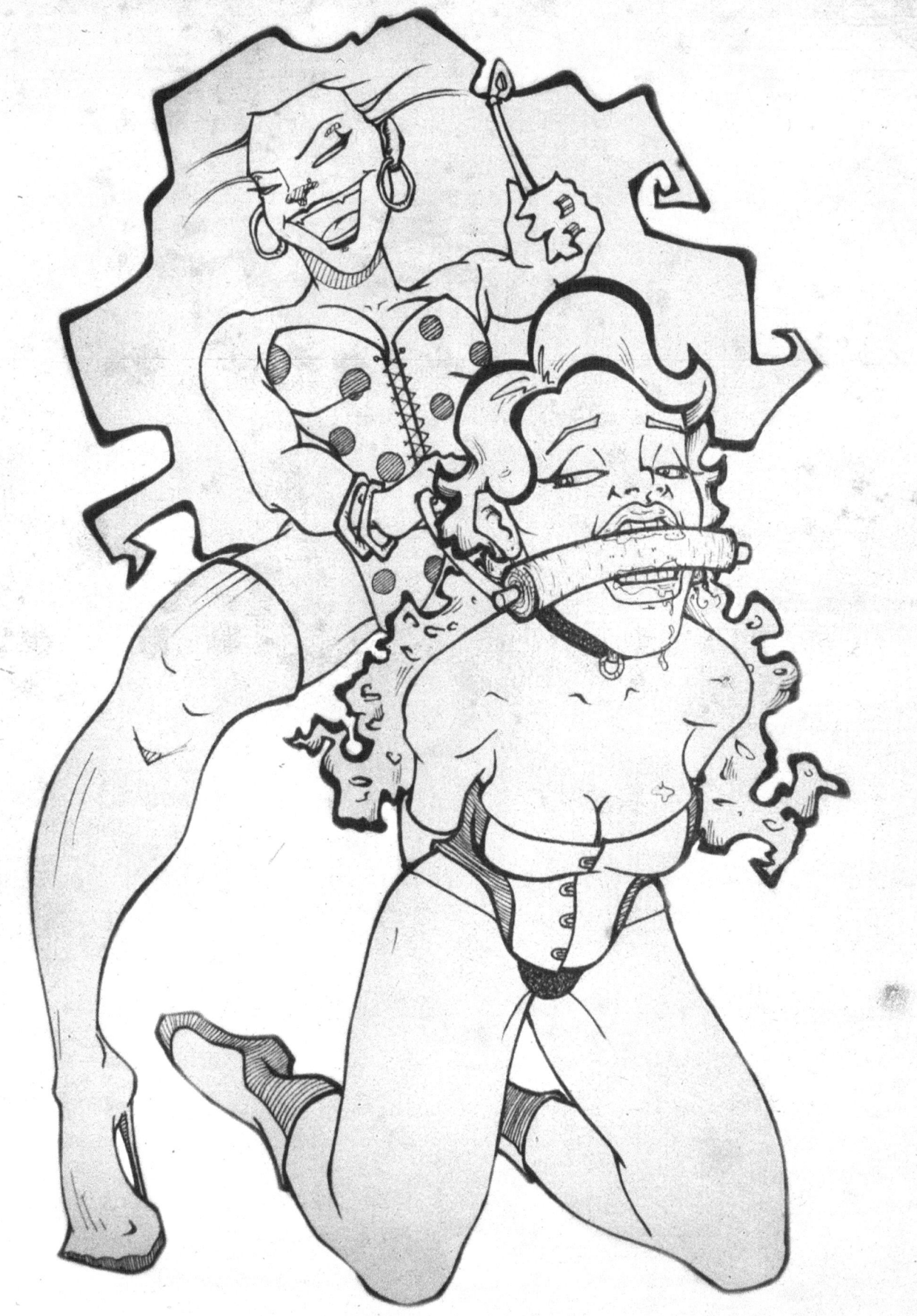

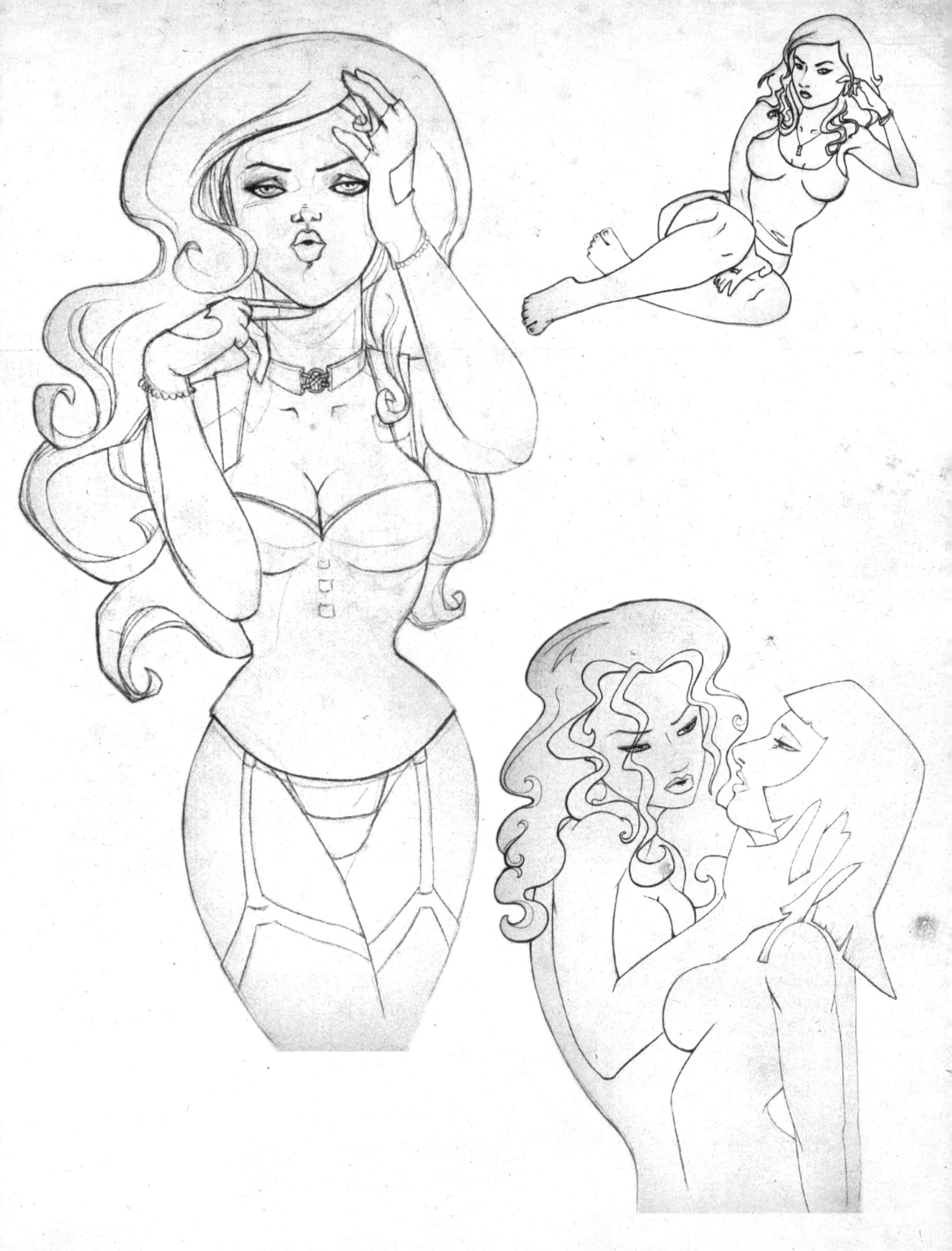

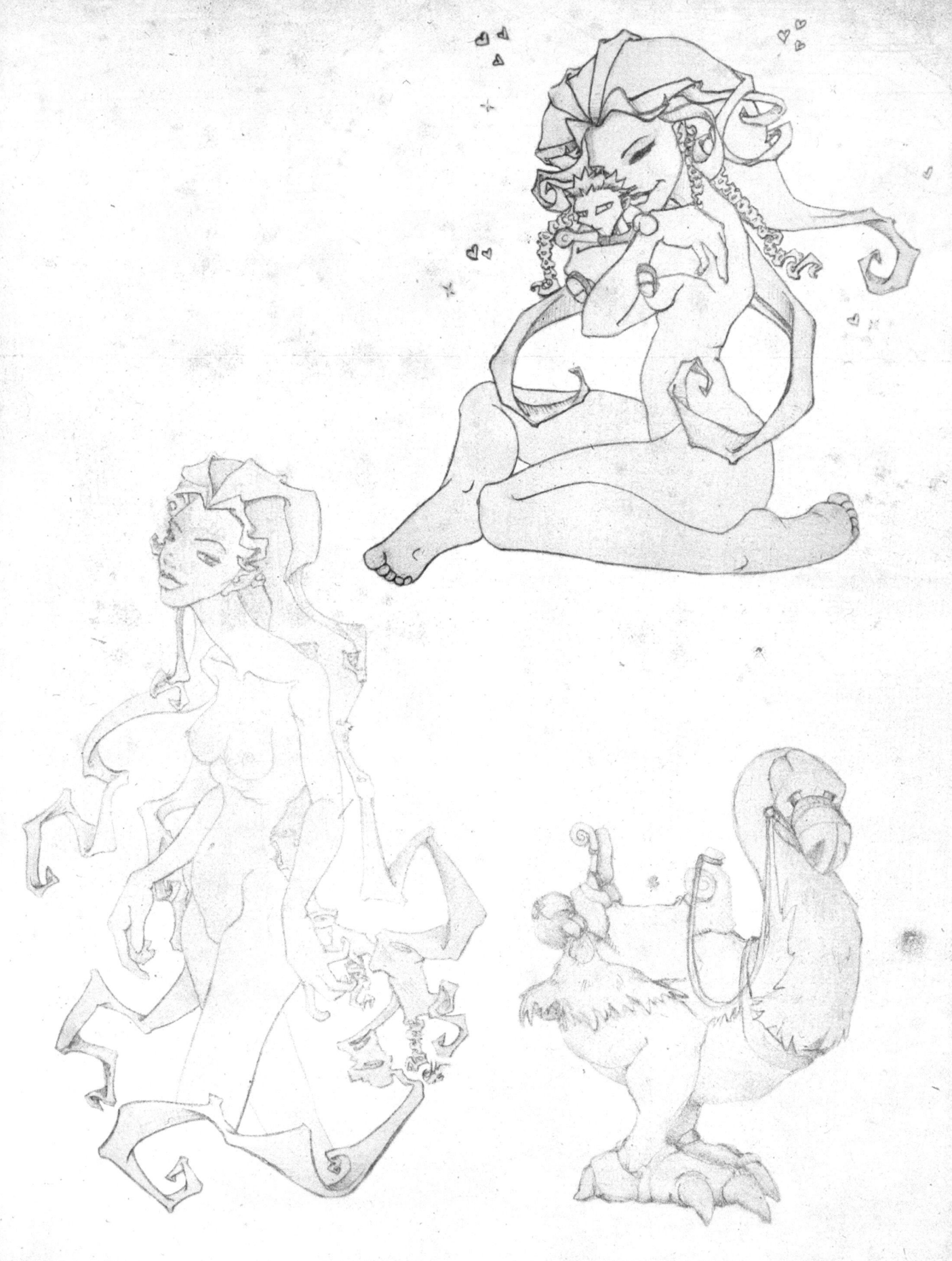

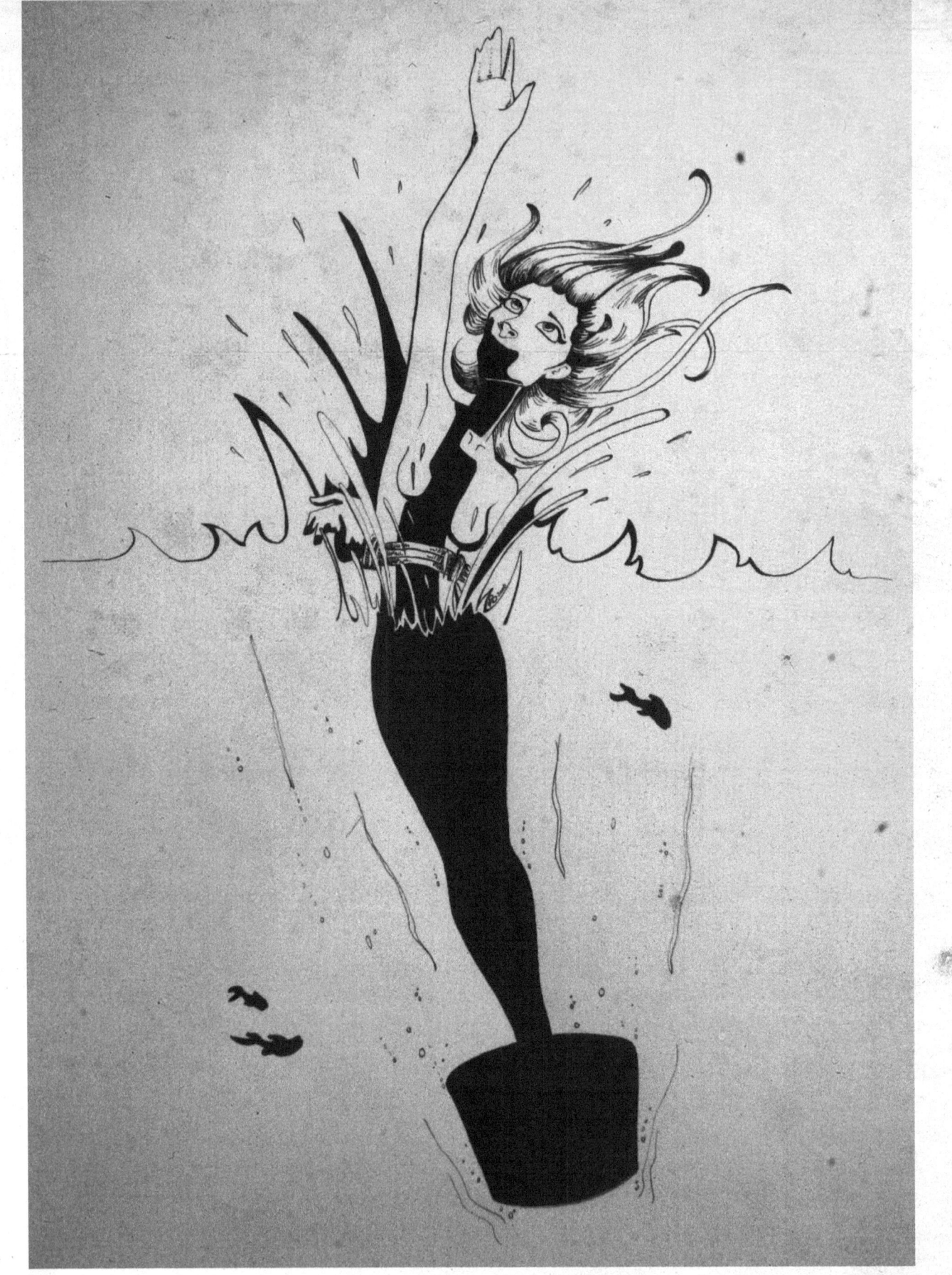

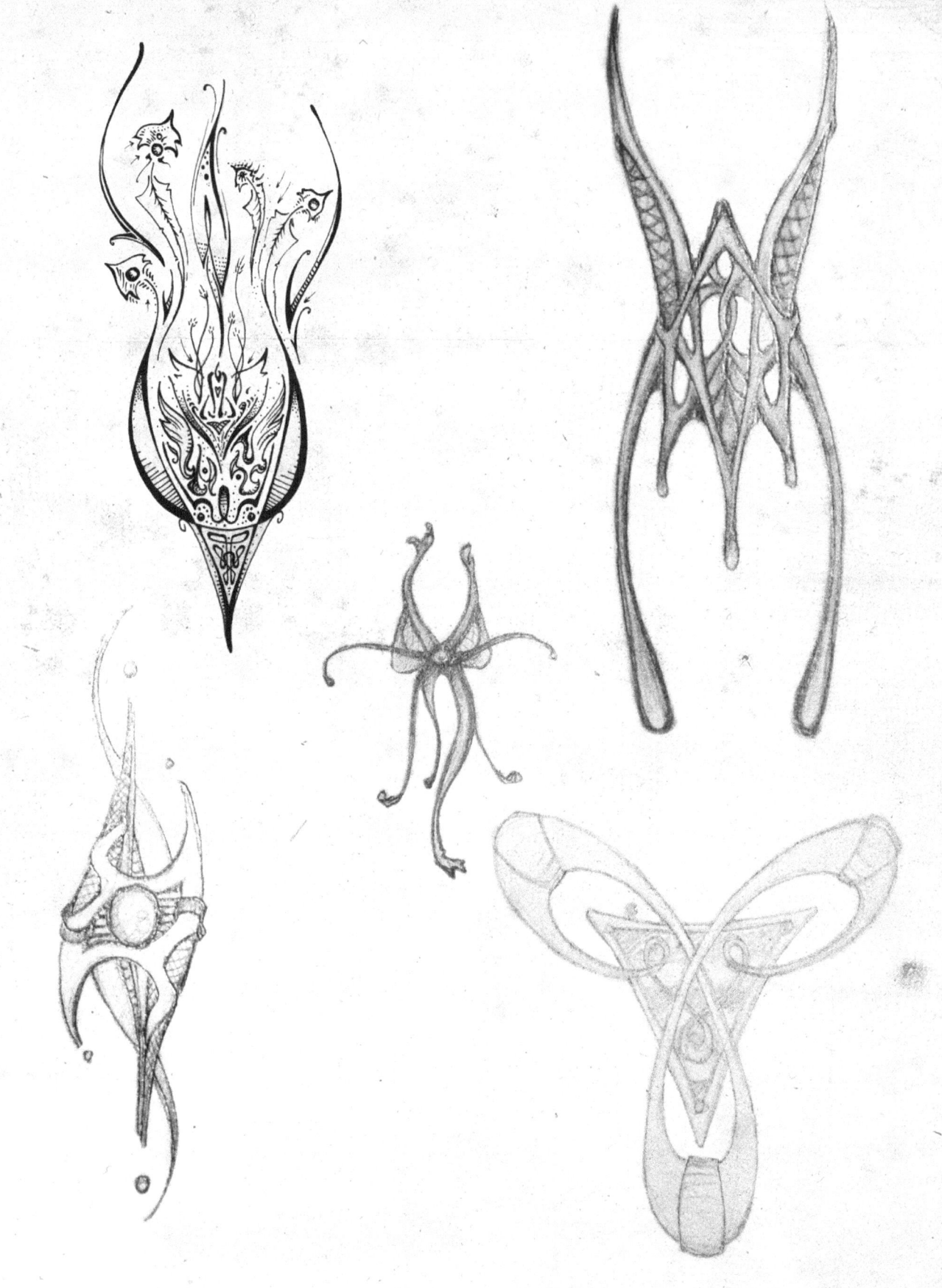

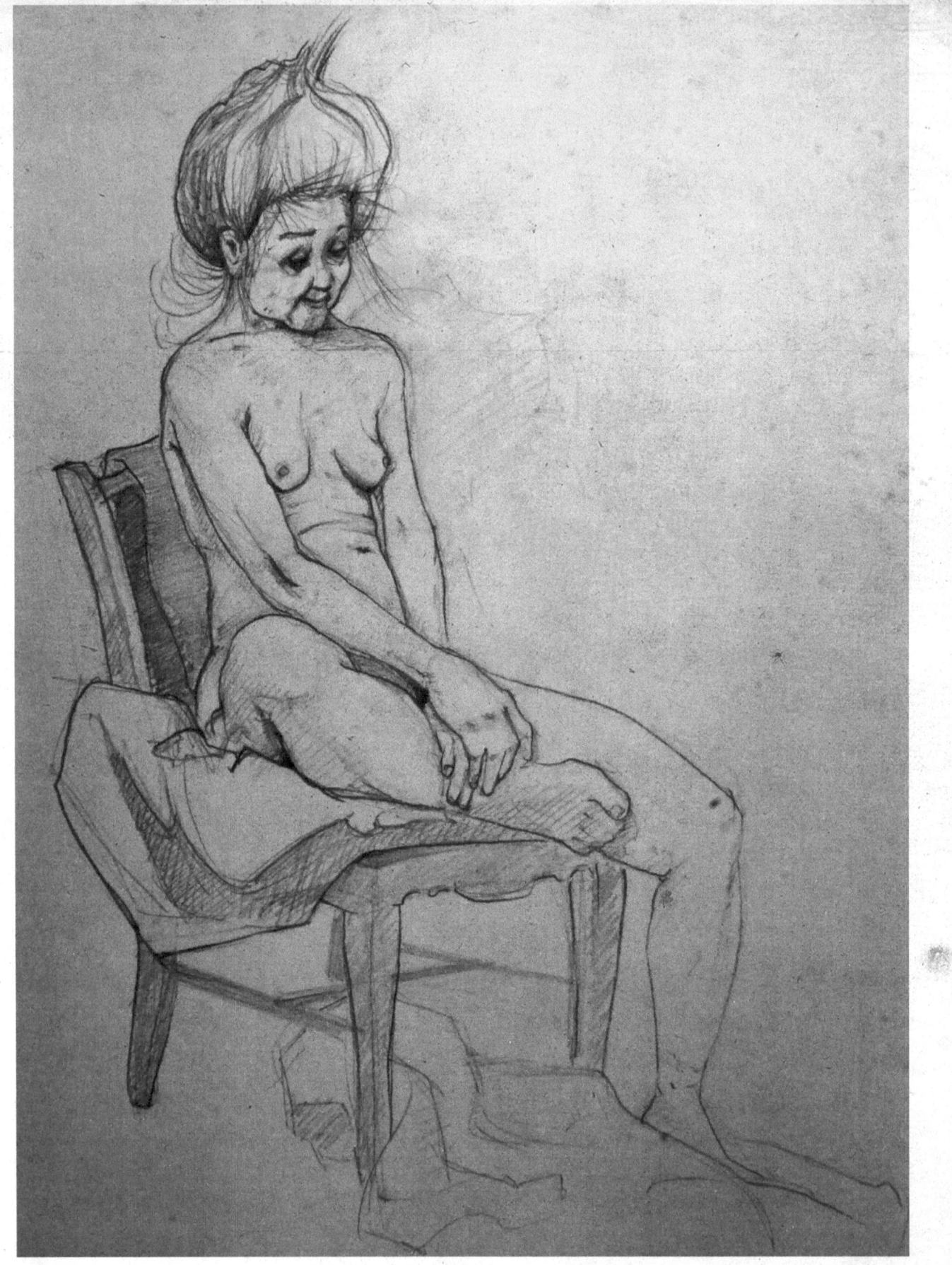

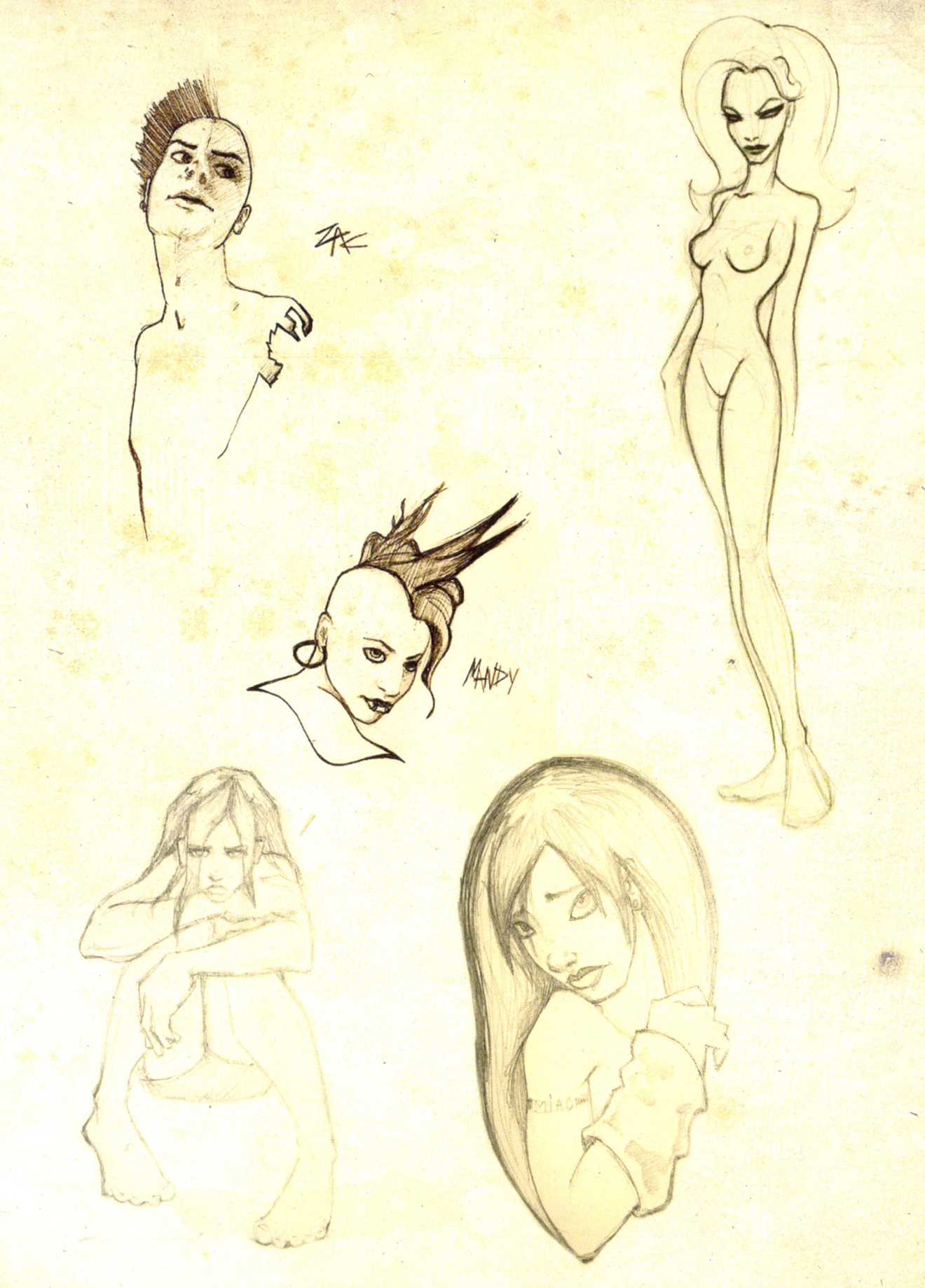

ZAC

MANDY

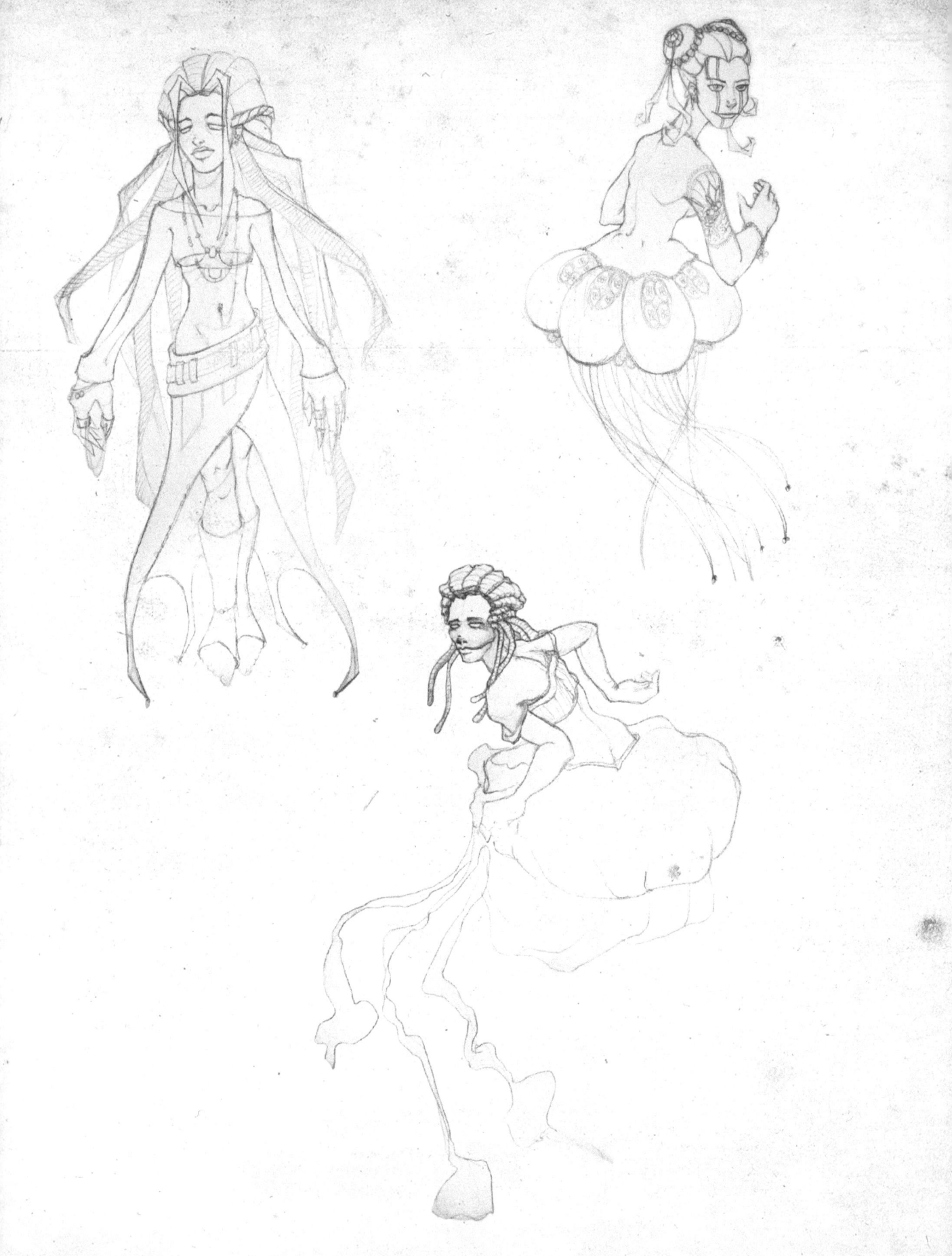

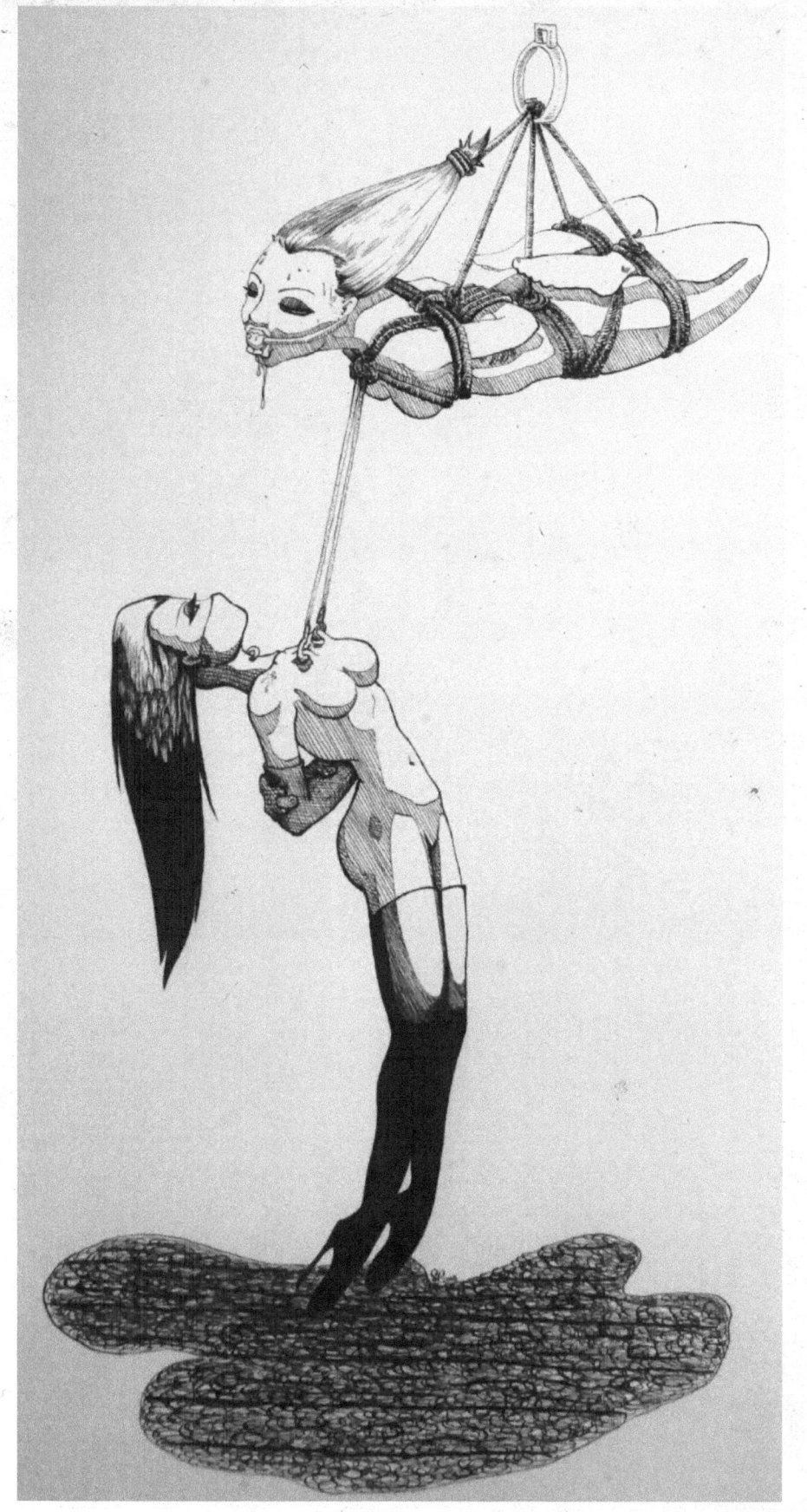

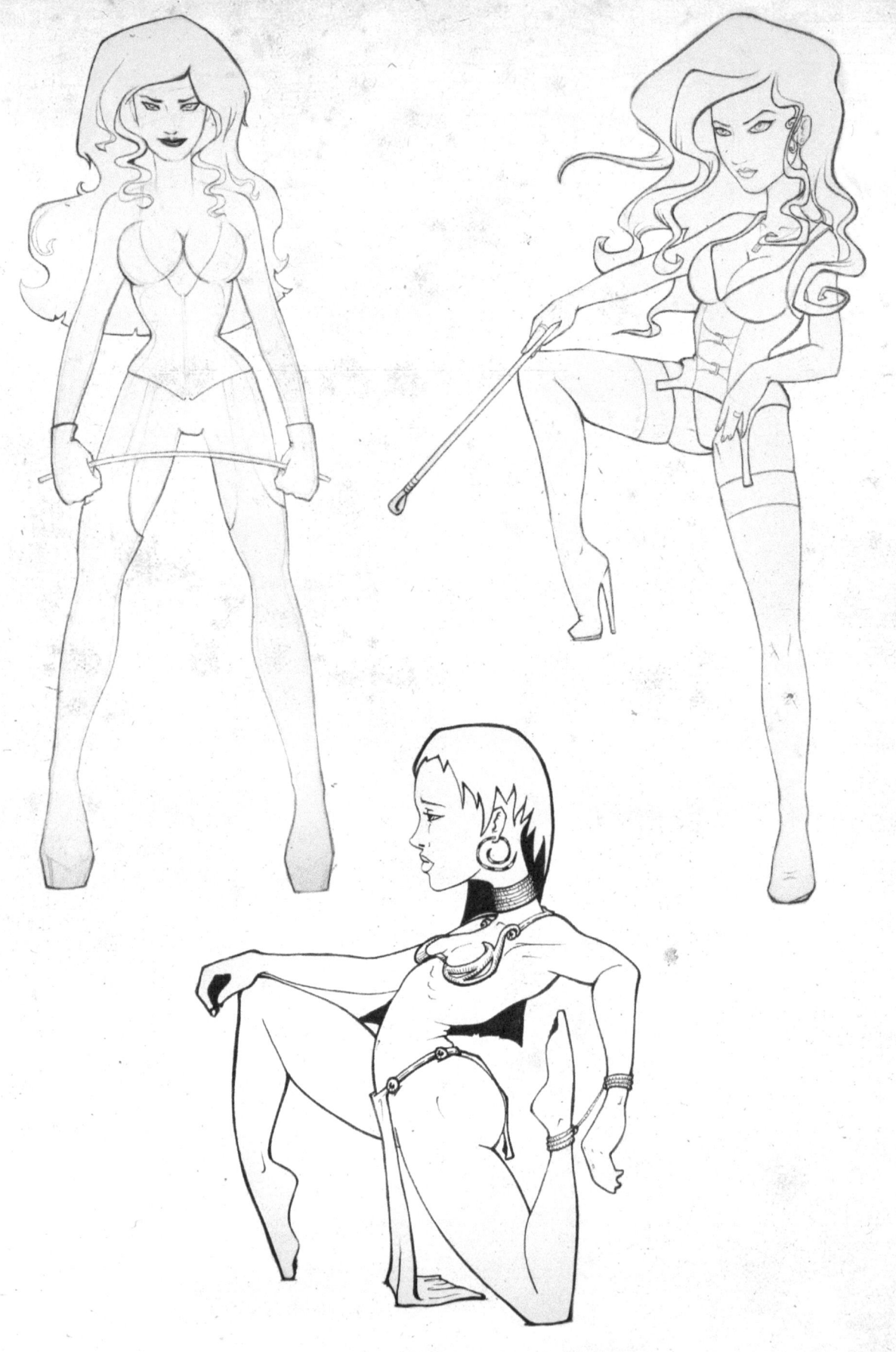

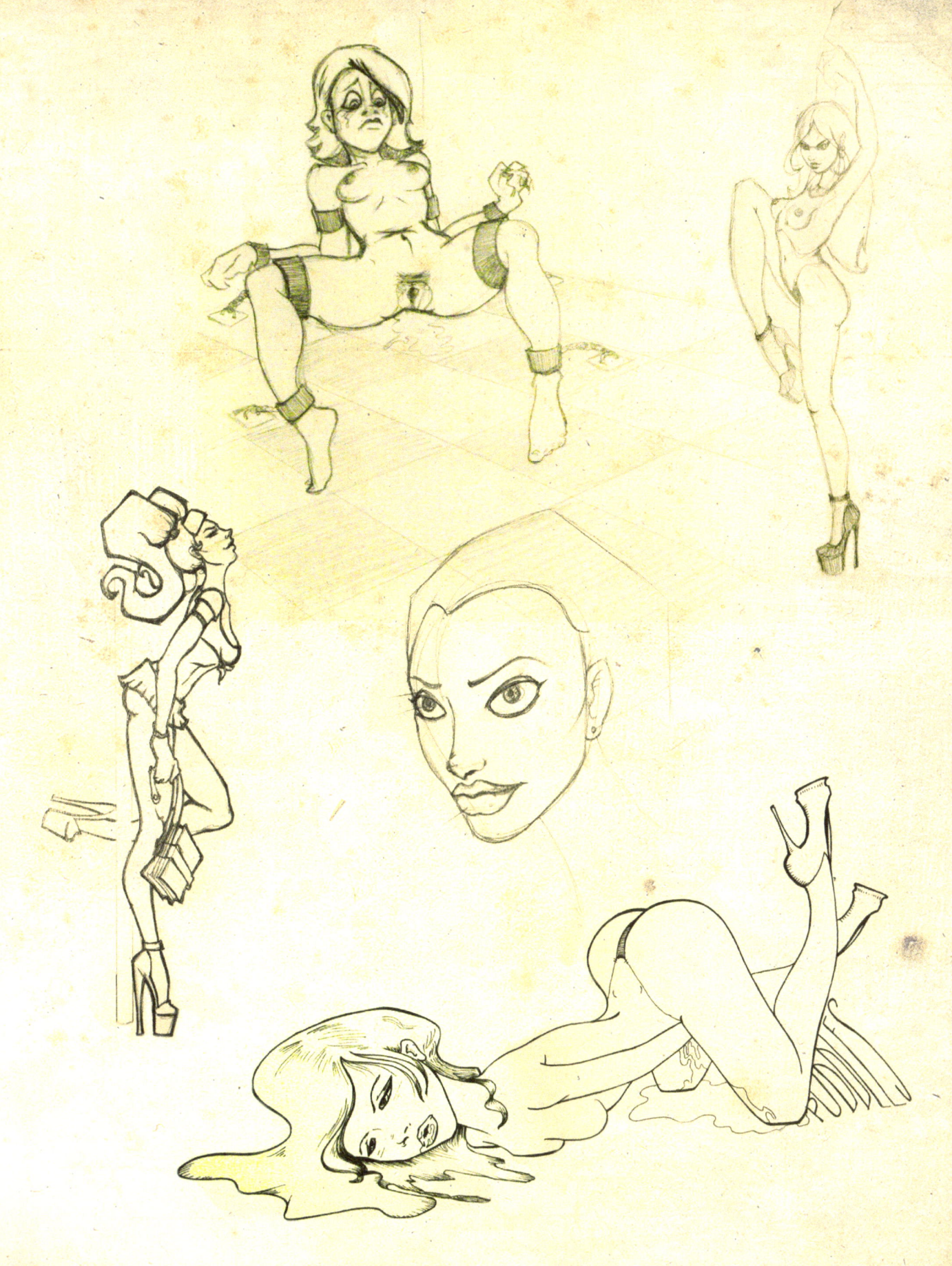

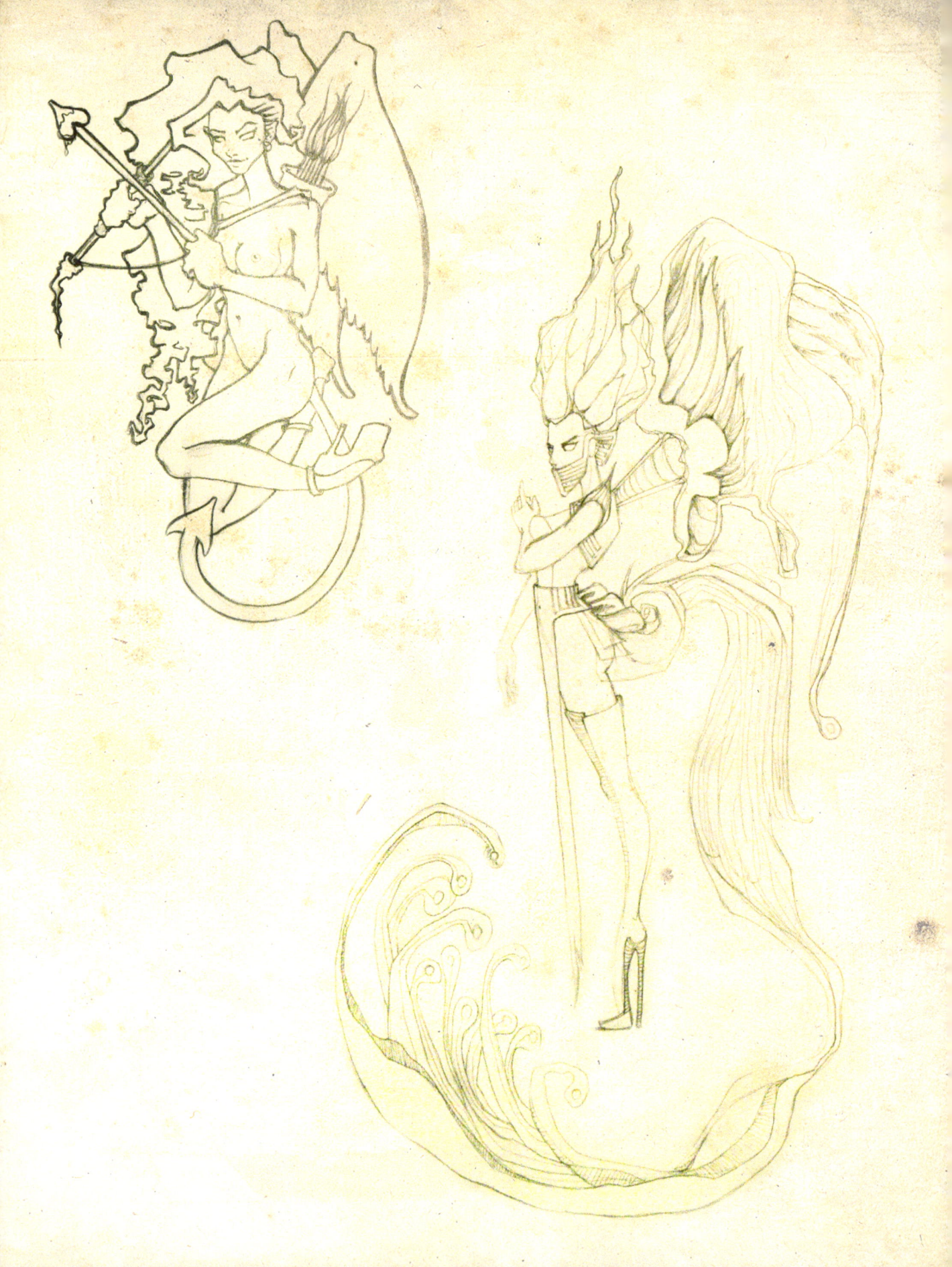

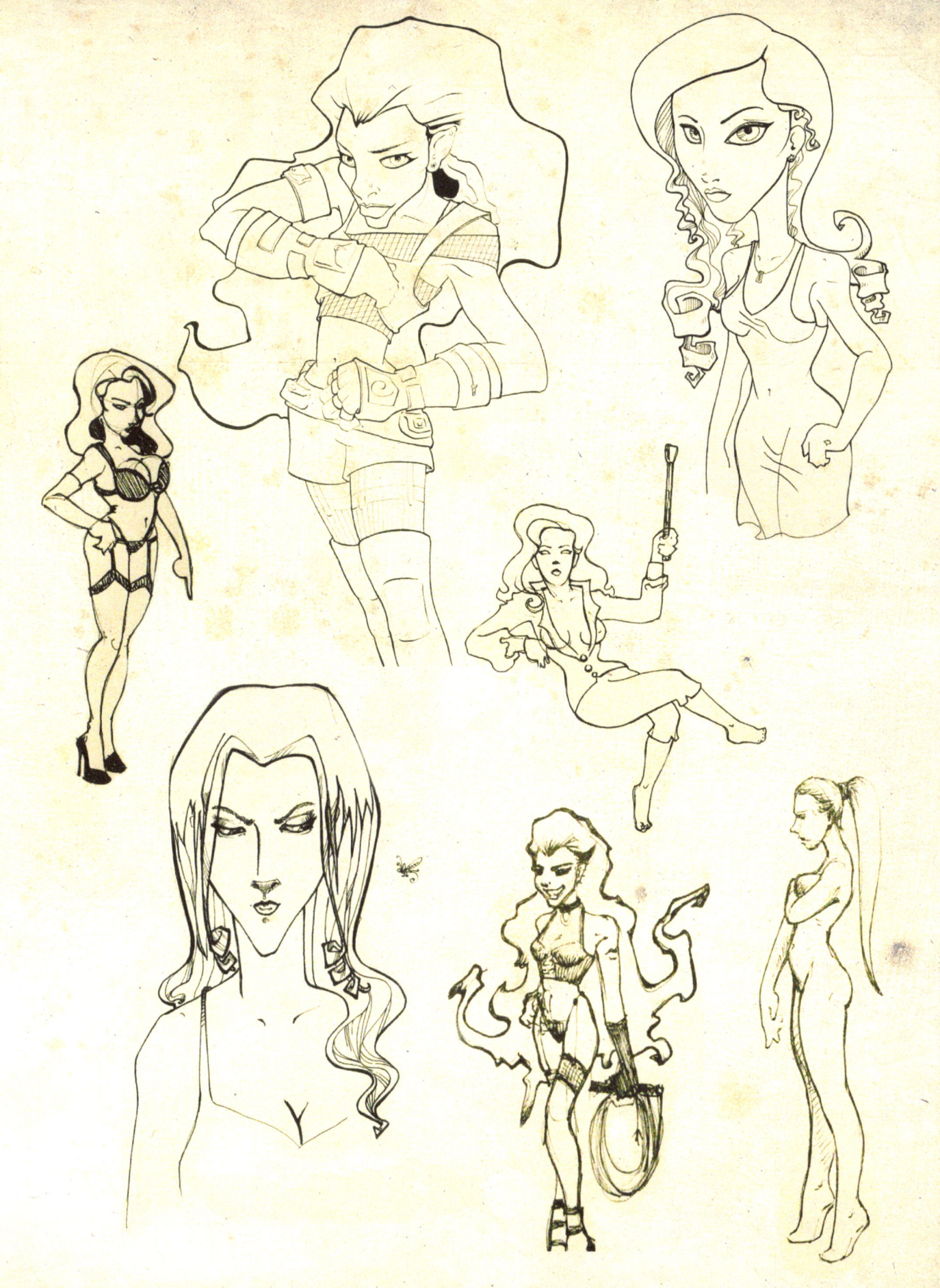

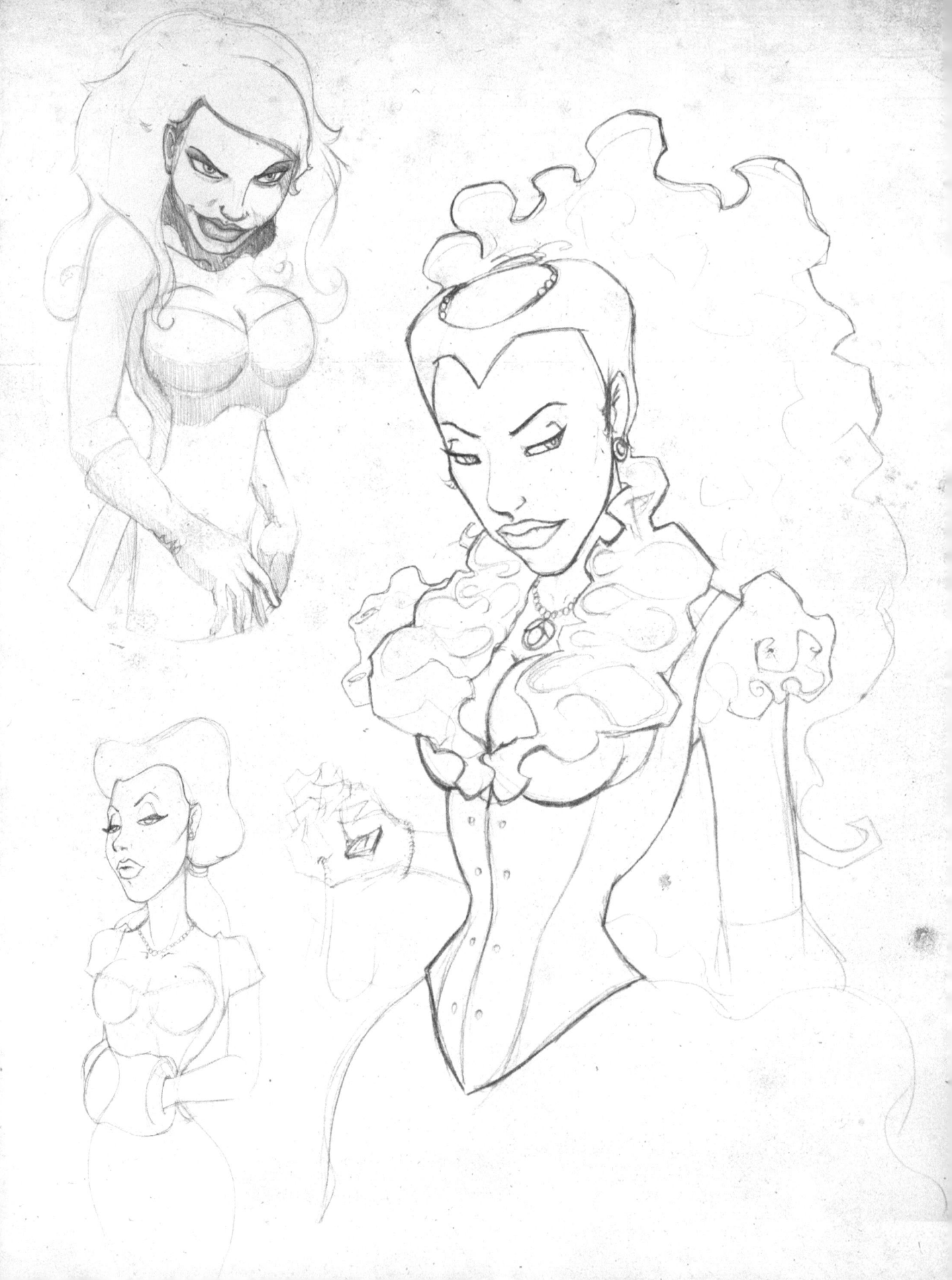

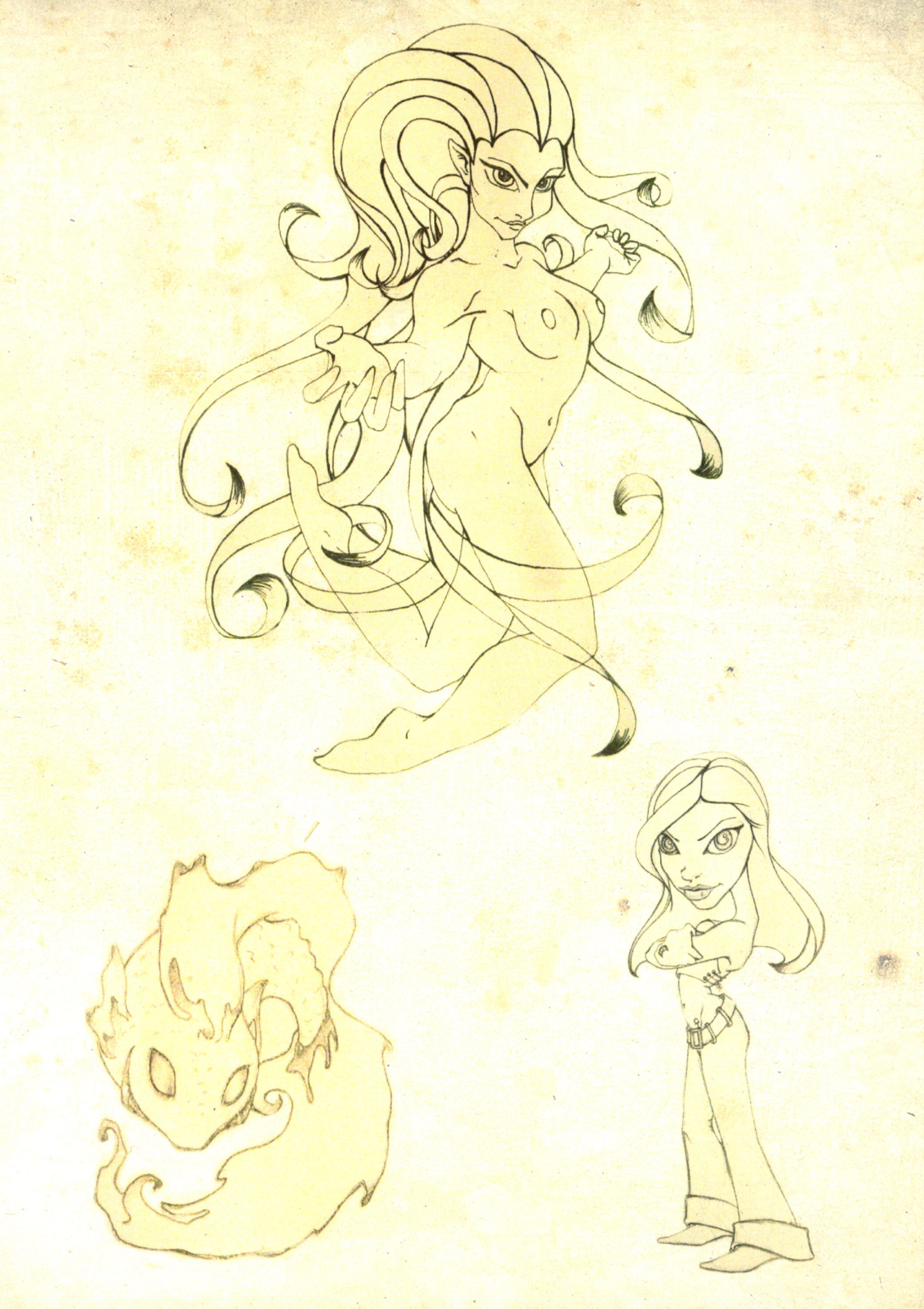

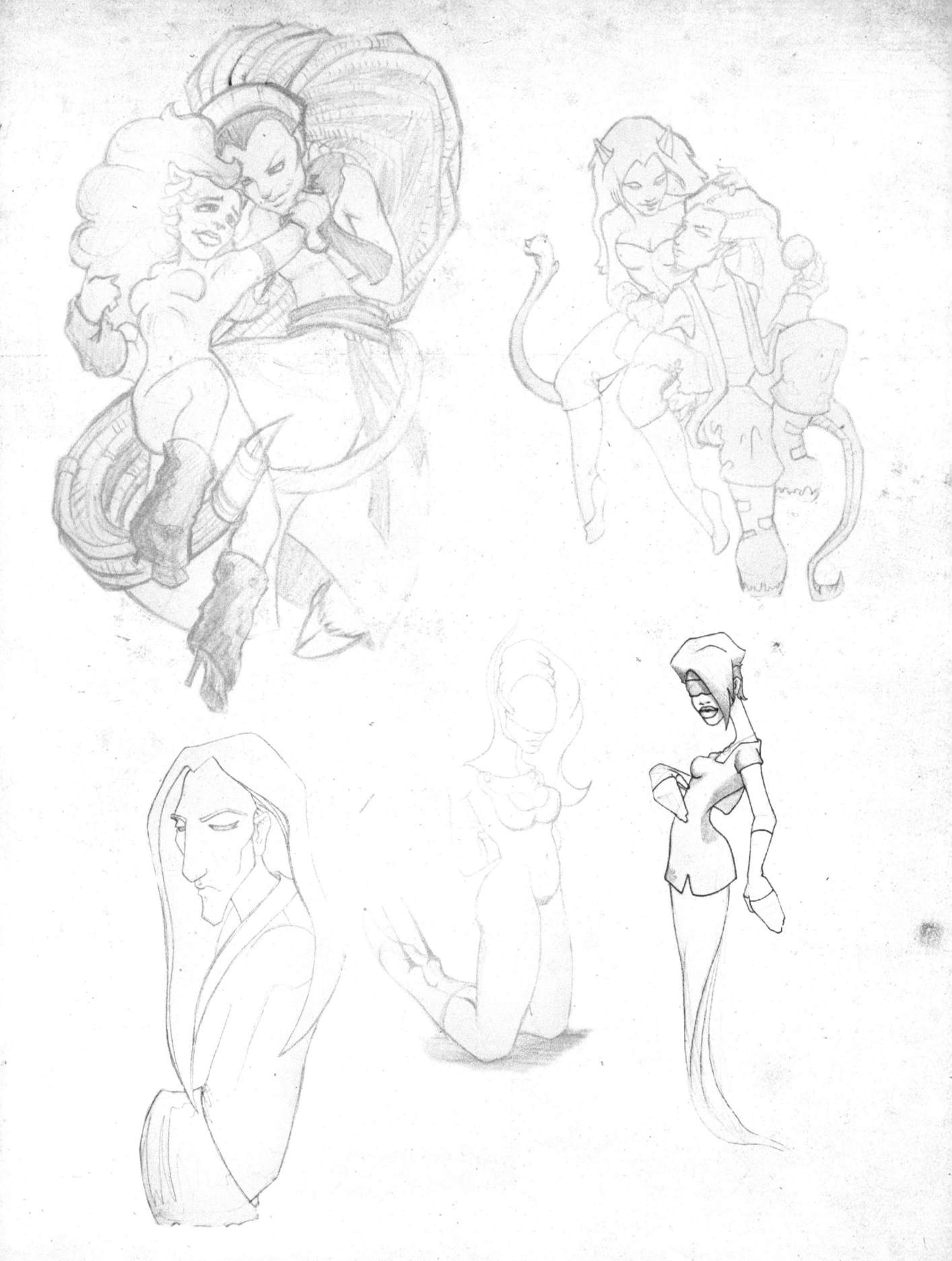

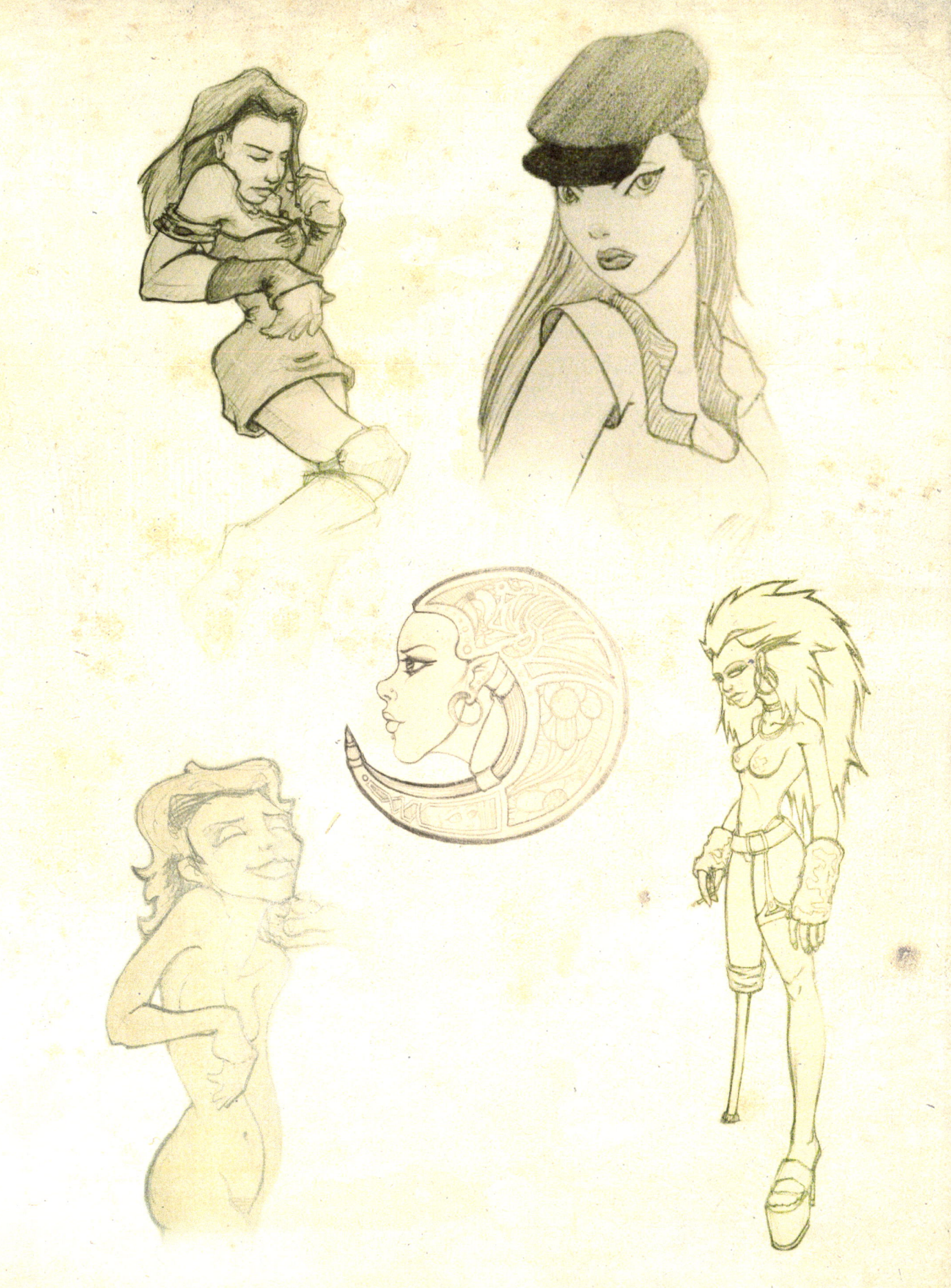

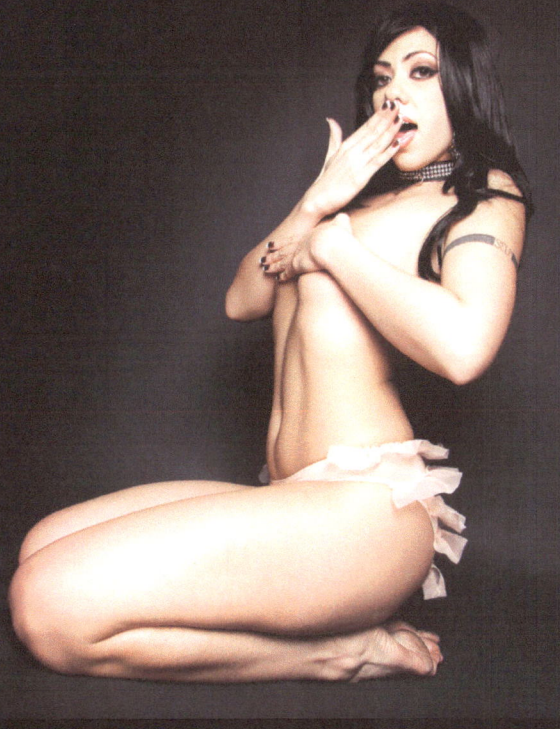

SATINE PHOENIX

FORMER PORN STAR & INTERNATIONAL
FETISH MODEL SATINE PHOENIX RETURNS
TO HER ROOTS AS A FETISH, COMIC BOOK
& CONCEPTUAL ARTIST.

FROM 1998 - 2002 SHE ATTENDED THE
ACADEMY OF ART UNIVERSITY (SAN
FRANCISCO) STUDYING 3D, 2D & STOP
MOTION ANIMATION THEN MOVING ON
TO SCULPTURE AND ILLUSTRATION.
REALIZING SHE COULD NEVER FULLY
UNDERSTAND THE COMPLEXITIES OF
HUMAN EMOTION WITHOUT LIVING FULLY
SHE QUIT SCHOOL AND FOLLOWED HER
FANTASIES INTO THE WORLD OF
STRIPPING, MODELING AND
PORNOGRAPHY. FOR 8 YEARS SHE
CULTIVATED HER EXPERIENCES AND HAS
RETURNED FULLY EQUIPPED TO SHARE
WHAT SHE HAS LEARNED THROUGH AS
MANY CREATIVE MEDIUMS AS SHE
POSSIBLY CAN.

YOU CAN FIND HER ONLINE AS
HEAD MISTRESS OF
HTTP://SEXFOODANDCOMICBOOKS.COM

OR VISIT HER PORTFOLIO AT
HTTP://SATINEPHOENIX.DEVIANTART.COM

ON TWITTER:
HTTP://TWITTER.COM/SATINEPHOENIX

www.ingramcontent.com/pod-product-compliance
Lightning Source LLC
Chambersburg PA
CBHW050815180526
45159CB00004B/1672